HUGO MÜNSTERBERG

PSYCHOLOGY

AND

LIFE

Elibron Classics
www.elibron.com

PSYCHOLOGY
AND LIFE

BY

HUGO MÜNSTERBERG

PROFESSOR OF PSYCHOLOGY IN HARVARD UNIVERSITY

𝔚estminster
ARCHIBALD CONSTABLE & CO.
2 WHITEHALL GARDENS

TO

MY OLD FRIEND

HEINRICH RICKERT

PROFESSOR OF PHILOSOPHY IN THE UNIVERSITY

OF FREIBURG (BREISGAU)

PREFACE

THE following volume contains six essays which have been brought before the public during the last year at very different opportunities. The paper on History was delivered as the presidential address before the New York meeting of the American Psychological Association, and was published in the "Psychological Review." That on Education was read before the Harvard Teachers' Association at their last Cambridge meeting and printed in the "Educational Review." The essay on Physiology is an extension of a paper read before the American Physiological Society in New York, and has not as yet been published. The three other papers appeared in the "Atlantic Monthly." That on Mysticism was read before the Buffalo meeting of the Unitarian Ministers' Institute, and before the Philosophical Department of Princeton University ; that on Art was written for the Detroit meeting of the American Drawing - Teachers' Association, and that on Real Life was an address to Wellesley College. Two other papers on educational problems which I have also published during the last year in the " Atlantic Monthly " series, the one under the title "The Danger from Experimental Psychology," and the other " The Teacher and the Laboratory," are not reprinted here because the one was chiefly the criticism of a book and the other a rejoinder to an attack, but they may be mentioned here as supplementary interpretations of my educational views.

While the six essays were thus presented at first to very various audiences, this book is in no way a chance collection of disconnected pieces. The contrary is true. They represent six chapters of a book which was from the first planned as a unity, and the separate publication of the special parts is merely accidental. The group should decidedly be taken as a whole. One fundamental thought controls the book, and each essay leads only from a different point to the same central conviction.

This chief aim is the separation of the conceptions of psychology from the conceptions of our real life. Popular ideas about psychology suggest that the psychological description and explanation of mental facts expresses the reality of our inner experience. It is a natural consequence of such a view that our ethical and æsthetical, our practical and educational, our social and historical views are subordinated to the doctrines of psychology. These papers endeavor to show that psychology is not at all an expression of reality, but a complicated transformation of it, worked out for special logical purposes in the service of our life. Psychology is thus a special abstract construction which has a right to consider everything from its own important standpoint, but which has nothing to assert in regard to the interpretation and appreciation of our real freedom and duty, our real values and ideals. The aim is thus a limitation of that psychology which wrongly proclaims its results as a kind of philosophy; but this limitation, which makes the traditional conflicts with idealistic views impossible, gives at the same time to the well-understood psychology an absolute freedom in its own field, and the whole effort is thus as much in the service of psychology itself as in the service of the rights of life. A scientific synthesis of the ethical idealism with the physiological psychology of our days is thus my purpose. Every unscientific and unphilosophical synthesis remains there necessarily an

insincere compromise in which science sacrifices
its consistency and idealism sacrifices its beliefs ;
it is the task of true synthesis to show how the
one includes the other, and how every conflict is
a misunderstanding.

The first paper gives the fundamental tone
and characterizes the problem of the whole book.
The second paper, on Physiology, develops the
real functions of a scientific psychology, and
defends its absolute freedom in the consistent
construction of theories of mind and brain. The
following three papers show in three important
directions, in art, education, and history, how
such a consistent psychology, even though most
radical, cannot interfere with the conceptions and
categories which belong to the activities of life
and to their historical aspect. The last paper
finally makes a test for this separation, showing
that just as psychology is not to interfere with
the conceptions of life, these latter must not
interfere with the conceptions of psychology ;
wherever this happens, the scientific aspect of
mental life goes over into mysticism.

The isolated appearance of the different essays
has made it necessary that each could be understood alone without presupposing the knowledge
of the foregoing papers ; frequent repetitions

were thus unavoidable. It would have been easy to eliminate these in reprinted form, and to link the papers so that each should presuppose acquaintance with the preceding parts. But I have finally decided not to change anything and to publish them again in a form in which every paper can be understood for itself, because I think that in a subject so difficult and so antagonistic to the popular view the chief points of the discussion can have impressive effect only if they are brought out repeatedly, always in new connections and from new points of view. They may be clear, perhaps, at a first reading, but may become convincing only when they are reached from the most different starting-points. If the axe does not strike the same spot several times, the tree will not fall.

It may appear still less excusable that whenever I have had to return to the same points, I have made use of the same expressions like stereotyped phrases. The effect would have been of course much prettier if I had applied a rich variety instead of such a monotony of terms. But it seems to me that in such complicated problems exactness and sharpness of the technical terms is the condition for clearness and consistency, which cannot be replaced by a more or less æsthetical enjoyment. I do not want to entertain by these papers, I want to fight; to fight against dangers which I see in our public life and our education, in art and science; and only those who intend serious and consistent thought ought to take up this unamusing book.

I say frankly, therefore, that this little volume is not written for those who kindly take an interest in the psychological discussions of the essays, but do not care for the philosophical part which belongs to every one. For such readers much more attractive treatises on the new psychology are abundant. And there is a second group of possible readers to whom also I should seal the little book if I had the power. I refer to those who heartily agree with my general conclusion that no conflict between science and the demands of life exists, but who base this attitude merely on feeling and emotion, and who thus dread the indirect method of abstract conceptions, all the more since they are not troubled by a demand for consistency in science. I have nothing in common with them; I am not a missionary of the Salvation Army. And, finally, I must warn still a third group whose existence I should not have suspected if it had not shown most vehement symptoms of life after the publication of some of my "Atlantic Monthly" papers. I have in mind those who consider a critical examination of the rights and limits of a science as an attack against that science, instead of seeing that it is the chief condition for a sound and productive growth ; the triumph through confusion is in the long run never a real gain for a science. Those who, perhaps with anger, perhaps with delight, consider my warning against a dangerous misuse of psychology, pedagogy, and so on, as an onslaught against psychology or pedagogy itself, certainly misunderstand my intentions.

Finally, I wish to express my thanks to the Assistant in the Psychological Laboratory of Radcliffe College, Miss Ethel Puffer, for the revision of my manuscript, and to the Assistant in the Psychological Laboratory of Harvard University, Dr. Robert MacDougall, for the revision of the proofs. It is needless to say that in spite of their helpful retouching of my language, the whole cast shows the style of the foreigner who is a beginner in the use of English, and who must thus seriously ask for the indulgence of the reader.

HUGO MÜNSTERBERG.

HARVARD UNIVERSITY, February, 1899.

CONTENTS

PSYCHOLOGY AND LIFE

I

The world of science and learning, as well as
the social world, has its alternating seasons and
its capricious fashions. Mathematics and philosophy, theology and physics, philology and history, each has had its great time; each was once
favored both by the leaders of knowledge and
by the crowd of imitating followers. The nine-
teenth century, which began with high philosophical inspirations, has turned decidedly toward
natural science; the description of the universe
by dissolving it into atomistic elements, and the
explanation of it by natural laws without regard
for the meaning and value of the world, has
been the scientific goal. But this movement
toward naturalistic dissolution has also gone
through several phases. It started with the
rapid development of physics and chemistry,
which brought as a practical result the wonderful
gifts of technique. From the inorganic world
scientific interest turned toward the organic
world. For a few decades, physiology, the science

of the living organism, enjoyed an almost unsur-
passed development, and brought as its practical
outcome modern medicine.   From the functions
of the single organism public interest has been
drawn to the problems of the evolution of the
organic world as a whole.   Darwinism has in-
vaded the educated quarters, and its practical
consequence has been rightly or wrongly a revo-
lution against dogmatic traditions.

Finally, the interests of the century have gone
a step farther, — the last step which naturalism
can take.   If the physical and the chemical, the
physiological and the biological world, in short
the whole world of outer experience, is atomized
and explained, there remains only the world of
inner experience, the world of the conscious
personality, to be brought under the views of
natural science.   The period of psychology, of
the natural science of the mental life, began.
It dawned ten, perhaps fifteen years ago, and
we are living in the middle of it.   No Edison
and no Roentgen can make us forget that the
great historical time of physics and physiology is
gone; psychology takes the central place in the
thought of our time, and overflows into all
channels of our life.   It began with an analysis
of simple ideas and feelings, and it has developed to an insight into the mechanism of the
highest acts and emotions, thoughts and creations.   It started by studying the mental life

of the individual, and it has rushed forward to the psychical organization of society, to social psychology, to the psychology of art and science, religion and language, history and law. It began with an increased carefulness of self-observation, and it has developed to an experimental science, with the most elaborate methods of technique, and with scores of great laboratories in its service. It started in the narrow circles of philosophers, and it is now at home wherever mental life is touched. The historian strives to-day for psychological explanation, the economist for psychological laws; jurisprudence looks on the criminal from a psychological standpoint; medicine emphasizes the psychological value of its assistance; the realistic artist and poet fight for psychological truth; the biologist mixes psychology in his theories of evolution; the philologist explains the languages psychologically; and while æsthetical criticism systematically coquets with psychology, pedagogy seems ready even to marry her.

As the earlier stages of naturalistic interests, the rush toward physics, physiology, biology, were each, as we have seen, of characteristic influence on the practical questions of real life, it is a matter of course that this highest and most radical type of naturalistic thinking, the naturalistic dissolution of mental life, must stir up and even revolutionize the whole practical world. From the nursery to the university, from the hospital to the court of justice, from the theatre to the church, from the parlor to the parliament, the new influence of psychology on the real daily life is felt in this country as in Europe, producing new hopes and new fears, new schemes and new responsibilities.

Let us consider the world we live in, from the point of view of this new creed. What becomes of the universe and what of the human race, what becomes of our duty and what of our freedom, what becomes of our friends and what of ourselves, if psychology is not only true, but the only truth, and has to determine the values of our real life?

II

What is our personality, seen from the psychological point of view? We separate the consciousness and the content of consciousness. From the standpoint of psychology, — I mean a consistent psychology, not a psychology that lives by all kinds of compromises with philosophy and ethics, — from the standpoint of psychology the consciousness itself is in no way a personality; it is only an abstraction from the totality of conscious facts, — an abstraction just as the conception of nature is abstracted from the natural physical objects. Consciousness does not do anything; consciousness is only the empty place for the manifoldness of psychical facts; it is the mere presupposition making possible the existence of the content of consciousness, but every thought and feeling and volition must be itself such a content of consciousness. Personality, too, is thus a content; it is the central content of our consciousness, and psychology can show in a convincing way how this fundamental idea grows and influences the development of mental life. We know how the whole idea of personality crystallizes about those tactual and muscular and optical sensations which come from the body; how at first the child does not discriminate his own limbs from the outside objects he sees; and how slowly the experiences, the pains, the successes, which connect themselves with the movements and contacts of this one body blur into the idea of that central object, our physical personality, into which the mental experiences become gradually introjected.

Psychology shows how this idea of the Ego grows steadily side by side with the idea of the Alter, and how it associates with itself the whole manifoldness of personal achievements and experiences. Psychology shows how it develops toward a sociological personality, appropriating everything which works in the world under the control of our will, in the interest of our influence, just as our body works, including thus our name and our clothing, our friends and our work, our property and our social community. Psychology shows how, on the other hand, this idea can shrink and expel everything which is not essential for the continuity of this central group of psychical contents. Our personality does not depend upon our chance knowledge and chance sensations; it remains, once formed, if we lose even our arms and legs with their sensations; and thus the personality becomes that most central group of psychical contents which accompany the transformation of experiences into actions; that is, feelings and will. Thus psychology demonstrates a whole scale of personalities in every one of us, — the psychological one, the sociological one, the ideal one; but each one is and can be only a group of psychical contents, a bundle of sensational elements. It is an idea which is endlessly more complicated, but theoretically not otherwise constituted, than the idea of our table or our house; just as, from the point of view of chemistry, the substance which we call a human body is theoretically not otherwise constituted than any other physical thing. The influence of the idea of personality means psychologically, then, its associative and inhibitory effects on the mechanism of the other contents of consciousness, and the unity and continuity of the personality mean that causal connection of its parts by which anything that has once entered our psychical life may be at any time reproduced, and may help to change the associative effects which come from the idea of ourselves.

Has this psychological personality freedom of will? Certainly. Everything depends in this case upon the definitions, and the psychologist can easily construct a conception of freedom which is in the highest degree realized in the psychophysical organism and its psychological experiences. Freedom of will means to him absence of an outer force, or of pathological disturbance in the causation of our actions. We are free, as our actions are not the mere outcome of conditions which lie outside of our organism, but the product of our own motives and their normal connections. All our experiences and thoughts, our inherited dispositions and trained habits, our hopes and fears, coöperate in our consciousness and in its physiological substratum, our brain, to bring about the action. Under the same outer conditions, somebody else would have acted otherwise; or we ourselves should have preferred and done something else, if our memory or our imagination or our reason had furnished some other associations. The act is ours, we are responsible, we could have stopped it; and only those are unfree, and therefore irresponsible, who are passive sufferers from an outer force, or who have no normal mental mechanism for the production of their action, a

psychophysical disturbance which comes as a
kind of outer force to paralyze the organism, be
it alcohol or poison, hypnotism or brain disease,
which comes as an intruder to inhibit the regular
free play of the motives.

Of course, if we should ask the psychologist
whether this unfree and that free action stand
in different relations to the psychological and
physiological laws, he would answer only with a
smile.   To think that freedom of will means in-
dependence of psychological laws is to him an
absurdity; our free action is just as much determined by laws, and psychologically just as
necessary, as the irresponsible action of the hypnotized or of the maniacal subject.   That the
whole world of mental facts is determined by
laws, and that therefore in the mental world
just as little as in the physical universe do wonders happen, is the necessary presupposition of
psychology, which it does not discuss, but takes
for granted.   If the perceptions, associations,
feelings, emotions, and dispositions are all given,
the action must necessarily happen as it does.
The effect is absolutely determined by the combination of causes; only the effect is a free
one, because those causes lay within us.   To be
sure, those causes and motives in us have themselves causes, and these deeper causes may not
lie in ourselves.   We have not ourselves chosen
all the experiences of our lives; we did not our-

selves pick out the knowledge with which our
early instruction provided us; we have not ourselves created those brain dispositions and talents
and tendencies which form in us decisions and
actions. Thus the causes refer to our ancestors,
our teachers and the surrounding conditions of
society, and with the causes must the responsibility be pushed backwards. The unhealthy
parents, and not the immoral children, are responsible; the unfitted teacher, and not the mis-
behaving pupil, should be blamed; society, and
not the criminal, is guilty. To take it in its
most general meaning, the cosmical elements,
with their general laws, and not we single mortals, are the fools!

III

The actions of personalities form the substance
of history. Whatever men have created by their
will in politics and social relations, in art and
science, in technics and law, is the object of the
historian's interest. What that all means, seen
through the spectacles of psychology, is easily
deduced. The historical material is made up
of will functions of personalities; personalities
are special groups of psychophysical elements;
free-will functions are necessary products of the
foregoing psychophysical conditions; history,
therefore, is the report about a large series of
causally determined psychophysical processes

which happened to occur. But it is a matter
of course that the photographic and phono-
graphic copy of raw material does not constitute
a science. Science has everywhere to go forward from the single unconnected data to the
general relations and connections. Consequently,
history as a scientific undertaking is not satisfied
with the kinematographic view of all the mental
processes which ever passed through human
brains, but it presses toward general connection,
and the generalizations for single processes are
the causal laws which underlie them. The aim
of history, then, must be to find the constant
psychological laws which control the development of nations and races, and which produce
the leader and the mob, the genius and the
crowd, war and peace, progress and social diseases. The great economic and climatic factors
in the evolution of the human race come into
the foreground; the single individual and the
single event disappear from sight; the extraordinary man becomes the extreme case of the
average crowd, produced by a chance combination of dispositions and conditions; genius
and insanity begin to touch each other; nothing
is new; the same conditions bring again and
again the same effects in new masks and gowns;
history, with all its branches, becomes a vast department of social psychology.

But if the free actions of historical personalities are the necessarily determined functions of psychophysical organisms, what else are and can be the norms and laws which these personalities obey? Certainly, the question which such laws answer, the question what ought to be, does not coincide with the question what is; but even that " ought " exists only as a psychical content in the consciousness of men, as a content which attains the character of a command only by its associative and inhibitory relations to our feelings and emotions. In short, it is a psychical content which may be characterized by special effects on the psychological mechanism of associations and actions, but which is theoretically coördinated to every other psychical idea, and which grows and varies, therefore, in human minds, under the same laws of adaptation and inheritance and tradition as every other mental thing. Our ethical laws are, then, the necessary products of psychological laws, changing with climate and race and food and institutions, types of action desirable for the conservation of the social organism. And just the same must be true for æsthetical and even for logical rules and laws. Natural processes have in a long evolutionary development produced brains which connect psychological facts in a useful correspondence to the surrounding physical world; an apparatus which connects psychical facts in a way which misleads in the outer physical world is badly adapted, and must be lost in the struggle for existence. Logical laws are, then, just so many types of useful psychical processes, depending upon the psychophysical laws, and changing with the conditions and complications of life.

The psychologist will add: Do not feel worried by that merely psychological origin of all our inner laws. Is not their final goal also in any case only the production of a special psychophysical state? What else can our thinking and feeling and acting strive for than to produce a mental state of agreeable character? We think logically because the result is useful for us; that is, secures the desired agreeable, practical ends. We seek beauty because we enjoy beautiful creations of art and nature. We act morally because we wish to give to others also that happiness which we desire for ourselves. In short, the production of the psychological states of delight and enjoyment in us and others, and the reduction of the opposite mental states of pain and sorrow, are the only aim and goal of a full, sound life. Were all the disagreeable feelings in human consciousness replaced by happy feelings, one psychological content thus replaced by another, heaven would be on earth.

But psychology can go one more step forward. We know what life means to it, but what does the world mean? What is its meta-

physical credo? There need not be much speculative fight about it. All who understand the
necessary premises of psychology ought to agree
as to the necessary conclusions. Psychology
starts with the presupposition that all objects
which have existence in the universe are physical
or psychical, objects in matter or objects in consciousness. Other objects are not perceivable
by us, and therefore do not exist. To come
from this to a philosophical insight into the ultimate reality, we must ask whether these physical
and psychical facts are equally true. To doubt
that anything at all exists is absurd, as such
a thought shows already that at least thoughts
exist. The question is, then, only whether both
physical and psychical facts are real, or physical
only, or psychical only. The first view is philosophical dualism; the second is materialistic
monism; and the third is spiritualistic monism.
Psychology cannot hesitate long. What absurdity to believe in materialism, or even in
dualism, as it is clear that in the last reality all
matter is given to us only as idea in our consciousness! We may see and touch and hear
and smell the physical world, but whatever we
see we know only as our visual sensations, and
what we touch is given to us as our tactual sensations; in short, we have an absolute knowledge
which no philosophical criticism can shake, only
in our own sensations and other contents of con-

sciousness. Physical things may be acknowledged as a practical working hypothesis for the simple explanation of the order of our sensations, but the philosophical truth must be that our psychical facts alone are certain, and therefore undoubtedly real.

Only our mind-stuff is real. Yet I have no right to call it "ours," as those other personalities whom I perceive exist also only as my perceptions; they are philosophically all in my own consciousness, which I never can transcend. But have I still the right to call that *my* consciousness? An I has a meaning only where a Thou is granted; where no Alter is there cannot be an Ego. The real world is, therefore, not my consciousness, but an absolutely impersonal consciousness in which a series of psychical states goes on in succession. Have I the right to call it a succession? Succession presupposes time, but whence do I know about time? The past and the future are given to me, of course, only by my present thinking of them. I do not know the past; I know only that I at present think the past; the present thought is, then, the only absolutely real thing. But if there is no past and no future, to speak of a present has no meaning. The real psychical fact is without time as without personality; it is for nobody, for no end, and with no value. That is the last word of a psychology which pretends to be philosophy.

IV

Now let us return to our starting-point : are we really obliged to accept this view of the world as the last word of the knowledge of our century? Can our historical and political, our ethical and æsthetical, our logical and philosophical thinking,—in short, can the world of our real practical life be satisfied with such a credo? And if we wish to escape it, is it true that we have to deny in our conscience all that the century calls learning and knowledge? Is it true that only a mysterious belief can overcome such positivistic misery, and that we have to accept thus the most anti-philosophical attitude toward the world which exists ; that is, a mixture of positivism and mysticism?

To be sure, we cannot, no, we cannot be satisfied with that practical outcome of psychology, with those conclusions about the final character of personality and freedom, about history and logic and ethics, about man and the universe. Every fibre in us revolts, every value in our real life rejects such a construction. We do not feel ourselves such conglomerates of psychophysical elements, and the men whom we admire and condemn, love and hate, are for us not identical with those combinations of psychical atoms which pull and push one another after psychological laws. We do not mean, with our responsibility and

with our freedom in the moral world, that our
consciousness is the passive spectator of psychological processes which go on causally determined
by laws, satisfied that some of the causes are
inside of our skull, and not outside.   The child
is to us in real life no vegetable which has to be
raised like tomatoes, and the criminal is no weed
which does not feel that it destroys the garden.

Does history really mean for us what psychological and economical and statistical laws put in
its place?   Are " heroism " and " hero-worship "
empty words?   Have Kant and Fichte, Carlyle
and Emerson, really nothing to say any more,
and are Comte and Buckle our only apostles?
Do we mean, in speaking of Napoleon and Wash-
ington, Newton and Goethe, those complicated
chemical processes which the physiologist sees in
their life, and those accompanying psychical processes which the psychologist enumerates between
their birth and their death?   Do we really still
think historically, if we consider the growth of
the nations and this gigantic civilization on earth
as the botanist studies the growth of the mould
which covers a rotten apple?   Is it really only a
difference of complication ?

But worse things are offered to our belief.
We are asked not only to consider all that the
past has brought as the necessary product of
psychological laws, but also to believe that all
we are striving and working for, all our life's

fight, — it may be the noblest one, — means nothing else than the production of some psychological states of mind, of some feelings of agreeableness ; in short, that the tickling sensations are the ideal goal of our life. The greatest possible happiness of the greatest possible number, that discouraging phrase in which the whole vulgarity of a naturalistic century seems condensed, is it really the source of inspiration for an ideal soul, and does our conscience really look out for titillation in connection with a majority vote ?

If you repeat again and again that there are only relative laws, no absolute truth and beauty and morality, that they are changing products of the outer conditions without binding power, you contradict yourself by the assertion. Do you not demand already for your skeptical denial that at least this denial itself is an absolute truth ? And when you discuss it, and stand for your conviction that there is no morality, does not this involve your acknowledgment of the moral law to stand for one's conviction ? If you do not acknowledge that, you allow the inference that you yourself do not believe that which you stand for, and that you know, therefore, that an absolute morality does exist. Psychological skepticism contradicts itself by its pretensions ; there is a truth, a beauty, a morality, which is independent of psychological conditions. When such ideal duties penetrate our life, we cannot rest at last in a psychological metaphysics where the universe is an impersonal content of consciousness; and every straightforward man, to whom the duties of his real life are no sounding brass, speaks with a calm voice to the psychologist: There are more things in heaven and earth than are dreamt of in your philosophy.

Is there really no possible combination of these two attitudes? Certainly such combination is not given by an inconsistent compromise. If we say to the intellect, Go on with your analyzing and explaining psychology, but stop halfway, before you come to practical acting; and say to our feeling and conscience, Go on with your noble life, but do not try to think about it, for all your values would show themselves as a poor illusion; then there remains only one thing doubtful, whether the conscience or the intellect is in the more pitiful state. Thinking that is too faint-hearted to act, and acting that is ashamed to think, are a miserable pair who cannot live together through a real life. No such coward compromise comes here in question, and still less do we accept the position that the imperfectness of the sciences of to-day must be the comfort of our conscience.

The combination of the two attitudes is possible; more than that, it is necessary in the right interests of both sides, as the whole apparent contradiction rests on an entire misunderstanding. It is not psychology that contradicts the demands of life, but the misuse of psychology. Psychology has the right and the duty to consider everything from the psychological standpoint, but life and history, ethics and philosophy, have neither the duty nor the right to accept as a picture of reality the impression which is reached from the psychological standpoint.

We have asked the question whether the psychical objects or the physical objects, or both, represent the last reality; we saw that dualistic realism and materialism decided for the last two interpretations, while psychology voted for the first. It seems that one of these three decisions must be correct, and just here is the great misunderstanding. No, all three are equally wrong and worthless; a fourth alone is right, which says that neither the physical objects nor the psychical objects represent reality, but both are ideal constructions of the subject, both deduced from the reality which is no physical object, no psychical object, and even no existing object at all, as the very conception of an existing object means a transformation of the reality. Such transformation has its purpose for our thoughts and is logically valuable, and therefore it represents scientific truth; but this truth nevertheless does not reach the reality of the untransformed life. It is exactly the same relation as that between natural science and materialism. Natural science considers the world as a mechanism, and for that purpose transforms the reality in a most complicated and ingenious way. It puts in the place of the perceivable objects unperceivable atoms which are merely products of mathematical construction quite unlike any known thing; and nevertheless these atoms are scientifically true, as their construction is necessary for that special logical purpose. To affirm that they are true means that they are of objective value for thought. But it is absurd to think, with the materialistic philosopher, that these atoms form a reality which is more real than the known things, or even the only reality, excluding the right of all not space-filling realities. The physical science of matter is true, and is true without limit and without exception; materialism is wrong from beginning to end. There is, indeed, no physical object in the world which natural science ought not to transmute into atoms, but no atom in the world has reality; and these two statements do not contradict each other.

In the same way psychology is right, but the psychologism which considers the psychological elements and their mechanism as reality is wrong from its root to its top, and this psychologism is not a bit better than materialism. It makes

practically no difference whether the real substance is of the clumsy space-filling material or
of the finer stuff that dreams are made of; both
are existing objects, both are combinations of
atomistic indivisible elements, both are in their
changes controlled and determined by general
laws, both make the world a succession of causes
and effects. The psychical mechanism has no
advantage over the physical one; both mean a
dead world without ends and values, — laws,
but no duties; effects, but no purposes; causes,
but no ideals.

There is no mental fact which the psychologist
has not to metamorphose into psychical elements;
and as this transformation is logically valuable,
his psychical elements and their associative and
inhibitory play are scientifically true. But a
psychical element, and anything which is thought
as combination of psychical elements and as
working under the laws of these psychical constructions, has as little reality as have the atoms
of the physicist. Our body is not a heap of
atoms; our inner life is still less a heap of ideas
and feelings and emotions and volitions and
judgments, if we take these mental things in the
way the psychologist has to take them, as contents of consciousness made up from psychical
elements. If it is understood that the function
of any naturalistic science is not to discover a
reality which is more real than our life and its

immediate battlefield, but only to transform the
reality in a special way, then it must be clear
that the demands of our real life can never be
contradicted by the outcome of the empirical
sciences.   The   sciences,   therefore, find their
way free to advance without fear till they have
mastered and transmuted the physical and the
psychical universe.

But we can go a step farther.   A contradiction is the more impossible since this transformation is itself under the influence of the elements
of real life, and by that the apparent ruler
becomes the vassal.   If psychology pretends
that there is no really logical value, no absolute
truth, because everything shows itself under
psychological laws, we must answer, This very
fact, that we consider even logical thinking
from the psychological point of view, and that
we have psychology at all, is only an outcome of
the primary truth that we have logical ends and
purposes.   Logical thinking creates psychology
for its own ends ; psychology cannot be itself
the basis for logical thinking.   And if psychology denies all values because they prove
to be psychical fancies only, we must confess
that this striving for the understanding of the
world by transforming it through our science
would have no meaning if it were not work
toward an end which we appreciate as valuable.
Every act of thought, every affirmation and

denial, every yes or no which constitutes a scientific judgment, is an act of a will which acknowledges the over-individual obligation to decide so, and not otherwise, — acknowledges an "ought," and works thus for duty. Far from allowing psychology to doubt whether the real life has duties, we must understand that there is no psychology, no science, no thought, no doubt, which does not by its very appearance solemnly acknowledge that it is the child of duties. Psychology may dissolve our will and our personality and our freedom, and it is constrained by duty to do so, but it must not forget that it speaks only of that will and that personality which are by metamorphosis substituted for the personality and the will of real life, and that it is this real personality and its free will which create psychology in the service of its ends and aims and ideals.

V

In emphasizing thus the will as the bearer of all science and thought, we have reached the point from which we can see the full relations between life and psychology. In the real life we are willing subjects whose reality is given in our will attitudes, in our liking and disliking, loving and hating, affirming and denying, agreeing and fighting ; and as these attitudes overlap and bind one another, this willing personality has unity. We know ourselves by feeling ourselves as those willing subjects; we do not perceive that will in ourselves; we will it. But do we perceive the other subjects? No, as little as ourselves. In real life, the other subjects also are not perceived, but acknowledged; wherever subjective attitudes stir us up, and ask for agreement or disagreement, there we appreciate personalities. These attitudes of the subjects turn toward a world of objects, — a world which means in real life a world of tools and helps and obstacles and ends; in short, a world of objects of appreciation

Do those subjects and their objects exist? No, they do not exist. I do not mean that they are a fairy tale; even the figures of the fairy tale are for the instant thought as existing. The real world we live in has no existence, because it has a form of reality which is endlessly fuller and richer than that shadow of reality which we mean by existence. Existence of an object means that it is a possible object of mere passive perception; in real life, there is no passive perception, but only active appreciation, and to think anything as object of perception only means a transmutation by which reality evaporates. Whatever is thought as existing cannot have reality. Our real will does not exist, either as a substance which lasts or as a process which is going on; but our will is valid, and has a form of reality which cannot be described because it is the last foothold of all description and agreement. Whoever has not known himself as willing cannot learn by description what kind of reality is given to us in that act of life; but whoever has willed knows that the act means something else than the fact that some object of passive perception was in consciousness; in short, he knows a reality which means more than existence.

The existing world, then, does not lack reality because it is merely a shadow of a world beyond it, a shadow of a Platonistic world of potentialities. No, it is a shadow of a real world, which stands not farther from us, but still nearer to us, than the existing world. The world we will is the reality; the world we perceive is the deduced, and therefore unreal system; and the world of potential forms and relations, as it is deduced from this perceivable system, is a construction of a still higher degree of unreality. The potentialities that form the only possible metaphysical background of reality are not the potentialities of existing objects, but the potentialities of will acts. This world of not existing but valid subjective will relations is the only world which history and society, morality and philosophy, have to deal with.

The willing subjects and their mutual relations are the only matter history can speak of, but not those subjects thought as perceivable existing objects; no, as willing subjects whose reality we can understand, not by describing their physical or psychical elements, but by interpreting and appreciating their purposes and means. The stones, the animals, even the savages, have no history; only where a network of individual will relations can be acknowledged by our will have we really history; and our own historical position means the system of will attitudes by which we acknowledge other willing subjects. To be sure, history, like every other science, must go from the raw material of single facts to generalities; but if we are in a world of not existing but valid realities, the generalities cannot be laws, but will relations of more and more general importance. Existing processes are scientifically generalized by laws; valid relations are generalized by more and more embracing relations. The aim of the real historian, therefore, is, not to copy the natural laws of physics and social psychology, but to work out the more and more general inner relations of mankind by following up the will influence of great men, till finally the philosophy of history shall comprise this total development from paradise to the day of judgment by one all-embracing will connection. Thus history in all its departments, history of politics and constitutions, of art and science, of language and law, has as its object the system of those human will relations which we ourselves as willing subjects acknowledge, and which are for us objects of understanding, of interpretation, of appreciation, even of criticism, but not objects of description and explanation, as they are valid subjective will functions, not existing perceivable objects.

History speaks only of those will acts which are acknowledged as merely individual. We know other will acts in ourselves which we will with an over-individual meaning, those attitudes we take when we feel ourselves beyond the domain of our purely personal wishes. The will remains our own, but its significance transcends our individual attitudes; it has an over-individual value; we call it our duty. To be sure, our duty is our own central will; there is no duty which comes from the outside. The order which comes from outside is force which seduces or threatens us; duty lies only in ourselves; it is our own will, but our will in so far as we are creators of an over-individual attitude.

If the system of our individual will acts is interpreted and connected in the historical sciences, the system of our over-individual will acts is interpreted and connected in the normative sciences, logic, æsthetics, ethics, and philosophy of religion. Logic treats of the over-individual will acts of affirming the world, æsthetics of those of appreciating the world, religion of those of transcending the world, ethics of those of acting for the world; and in virtue of this attitude also are constituted all the side branches of ethics, as jurisprudence and pedagogy. All treat of over-individual valid will relations, and no one has therefore directly to deal with existing psychical objects. On the basis of these normative sciences the idealistic philosophy has to build up its metaphysical system, which may connect the disconnected will attitudes of our ethical, æsthetical, religious, and logical duties in one ideal dome of thoughts. But however we may formulate this logically ultimate source of all reality, we know at least one thing surely, that we have deprived it of all meaning and of all values and of all dignity, if we picture it as something which exists. The least creature of all mortals, acknowledged as a willing subject, has more dignity and value than even an almighty God, if he is thought of merely as a gigantic psychological mechanism; that is, as an object the reality of which has the form of existence.

VI

How do we come, then, to the idea of existing objects? There is no difficulty in understanding that. Our life is will, and our will has its duties; but every action turns toward those means and obstacles and ends, those objects of appreciation, which are material for our will and our duties. Every act is thus a coöperation of subjects and subjectively appreciated objects; we cannot fulfill our duty, therefore, if we do not know what we have to expect from the objects in this coöperation. There must arise, then, the will to isolate our expectation about the objects; that is, to think what we should have to expect from the objects if they were independent of the willing subjects. In reality, they are never independent; in our thoughts, we can cut them loose from the willing subjects, and think of them as objects which are not any more objects of appreciation, but objects of perception only. These objects in their artificial separation from the real subject, thought of as objects of a passive spectator, take by that change a form which we call existence, and it is the aim of natural science to study these existing things. The path of their study is indicated to them by the goal they try to reach. They have to determine the expectations the objects bring up; at first, therefore, they look out for those features of the objects which suggest the different expectations, and natural science calls these features of the objects their elements. These elements are not really in the objects, but they represent all that which determines the possible variations of the objects in the future. Thus science considers the present thing a combination of elements to determine its relation to the future thing; but the present thing is, then, itself the future of the past thing, and it stands, in consequence, between past and future; that is, as a link in a chain in which everything is determining the future and determined by the past, everything cause and everything effect.

Natural science finds in this attempt that there may be two classes of such existing objects: objects which are possible, perceivable objects for every subject, and others which are perceivable only for one subject. Natural science calls the first group physical objects, the second group psychical objects, and separates the study of them, as this relation to the one or the many brings with it numerous characteristic differences, the differences between physics and psychology. But the point of view for both is exactly the same; both consider their material as merely perceivable objects which are made up from elements, and which determine one another by causal connections. Since they are thought as cut loose from the attitude of the will, neither the physical nor the psychical objects can have values or teleological relations.

But the will itself? If psychology, like physics, deals with the objects of the world in their artificial separation from the will, how can the will itself be an object of psychology? The presupposition of this question is in some way wrong; the will is primarily not at all an object of psychology. The real psychological objects are the ideas of our perception and memory and imagination and reason. Only if psychology progresses, it must come to the point where it undertakes to consider every factor of our mental life from a psychological point of view; that is, as an object made up from atomistic elements which the psychologist calls sensations. The will is not a possible object; psychology must make a substitution, therefore; it identifies the real personality with the psychophysical organism, and calls the will the set of conditions which psychologically and physiologically determines the actions of this organism. Now this will, too, is made up of sensations, — muscle sensations and others; and this will depends upon psychological laws, is the effect of conditions and the cause of effects; it is ironed with the chains of natural laws to the rock of necessity. The real will is not a perceivable object, and therefore neither cause nor effect, but has its meaning and its value in itself; it is not an exception to the world of laws and causes; no, there would not be any meaning in asking whether it has a cause or not, as only existing objects can belong to the series of causal relations. The real will is free, and it is the work of such free will to picture, for its own purposes, the world as an unfree, a causally connected, an existing system; and if it is the triumph of modern psychology to master even the best in man, the will, and to dissolve even the will into its atomistic sensations and their causal unfree play, we are blind if we forget that this transformation and construction is itself the work of the will which dictates ends, and the finest herald of its freedom.

Of course, as soon as the psychologist enters into the study of the will, he has absolutely to abstract from the fact that a complicated substitution is the presupposition for his work. He has now to consider the will as if it were really composed of sensational elements, and as if his analysis discovered them. The will is for him really a complex of sensations; that is, a complex of possible elements of perceptive ideas. As soon as the psychologist, as such, acknowledges in the analysis of the will a factor which is not a possible element of perception, he destroys the possibility of psychology just as much as the physicist who acknowledges miracles in the explanation of the material world denies physics. There is nothing more absurd than to blame the psychologist because his account of the will does not do justice to the whole reality of it, and to believe that it is a climax of forcible arguments against the atomizing psychology of to-day if philosophers exclaim that there is no real will at all in those compounds of sensations which the psychologist substitutes. Certainly not, as it was just the presupposition of psychology to abstract from that real will. It is not wiser than to cast up against the physicist that his moving atoms do not represent the physical world because they have no color and sound and smell. If they sounded and smelled still, the physicist would not have fulfilled his purpose.

Psychology can mean an end, and can mean also a beginning. It may be, and in this century, indeed, has been, the last word of a naturalistic attitude toward the world, — an attitude which emphasized only what is expected from the objects, and neglected the duties of the subjects. But psychology degenerates into an unphilosophical psychologism, just as natural science degenerates into materialism, if it does not understand that it works only from one side, and that the other side, the reality which is not existence, and therefore no possible object of psychology and natural science, is the primary reality. Psychology may be also a beginning. It can mean that we ought to abandon exaggerated devotion for the physical world, that we ought to look out for our inner world; a good psychology is then the most important supplement to those sciences which consider the inner life, not as an existing, describable, explainable object, but as a will system to be interpreted and to be appreciated. If that is the attitude, the psychological sciences on the one side, the historical and normative sciences on the other side, can really do justice to the totality of the problems of the inner life. If psychology tries to stand on both sides, its end must be near; the real life will tear it up and rend it in pieces. If it stands with strong feet on the one side, and acknowledges the right of the other side, it will have a future. The psychology of our time too often seems determined to die out in psychologism; that must be stopped. Psychology is an end as the last word of the naturalistic century which lies behind us; it may become a beginning as the introductory word of an idealistic century to be hoped for.

PSYCHOLOGY AND PHYSIOLOGY

I

In the opinion of the public the most characteristic feature of the present psychology is its association with physiology ; the questions in regard to the mind, which in earlier times belonged to the domains of the philosopher only, are now to be answered by inquiries as to the functions of the brain. This new situation has everywhere stirred up feelings of hope and feelings of fear ; the hope in the hearts of enthusiastic admirers of natural science, the fear in the souls of those for whom the ethical values of life stand foremost. Each of these two antagonistic feelings is based on a popular doctrine, and these two doctrines have absolutely nothing in common beyond the one fact that both are equally mistaken.

The hope-inspiring theory of the progressive friends of psychology is that brain physiology alone can teach us the real constitution of mental life, as the brain is a perceivable, palpable thing which can be dissected and microscopically examined, while the soul is a merely hypothetical construction of the metaphysicians. All the so-called knowledge of psychical life must thus be vague and foggy, and all exact and scientific knowledge of it must thus date from the time when the ganglion cells and association fibres were discovered to be the causes of mental action. The fear-suggesting theory of the more conservative friends of psychology does not deny that many psychical acts are dependent upon bodily functions, but while the others welcome the fact as an instrument of science, they despise it as an obstacle to an ethical life. All our duties depend upon the freedom of our decisions, and if it can be shown that our whole mental life is determined by the physiological processes in our brain, then the claim of freedom is meaningless; we stand then fully under the mechanical laws which move the molecules in our body. The necessary and logical consequence is that it must be a gain for morality to show that at least some psychical functions, the feelings for instance, or the attention or the volitions, may be independent of intermingling ganglion cells. The first view thus leads naturally to the wish to find as many relations between mind and brain as possible; the second view must lead to the opposite wish that such relations may finally be recognized as incomplete and full of exceptions.

The mistake of the psychophysiological enthusiasts lies more on the surface than that of the accusers. We are told that we are to expect an exact knowledge of the psychical facts from our knowledge of the brain; but what in the world can we know better than the objects of our immediate self-observation? The observation and analysis of our mental facts is in no way dependent upon a hypothesis in regard to the soul; it is the most direct object of our attention, and we thus know endlessly more about our psychical facts than about the functions of the brain. Even two thousand years ago the chief mental facts were well known, while the most fundamental questions of brain physiology are still to-day under lively discussion. Above all, the history of science shows how in the times of their coöperation psychology always had to give and physiology to take; light had to be thrown from the side of the well-known psychological facts upon the obscure physiological facts, and never in the opposite direction. The consequence of this situation is that psychologists in their work of analysis and research into the constitution of the psychical facts have not the slightest reason for inquiring into any accompanying brain processes; they cannot learn from that side anything which they do not know better from self-observation and the observation of others. Whether a special mental act occurs in one part of the brain or in another, whether

the cells or the fibres are engaged, whether the
processes are similar to the physical movements
in an electric wire or to the physiological actions
in an amœboid organism, whether the sensory
and motor centres are separate or identical, and
a hundred similar questions which stand in the
foreground of interest for the doctrine of psychophysiological relations are all equally indifferent for the study of the psychical facts as
such.   The increase of scientific exactitude must
come from the use of more refined methods in
self-observation, and all the work done in our
modern laboratories of experimental psychology
is in the service of this endeavor, while the
methods of histology and comparative anatomy,
of pathology and vivisectional physiology, all
indispensable for the psychophysiological problems, are unknown, and ought to remain unknown, in our psychological laboratories.   The
hope that physiological psychology will give us
a fuller acquaintance with the psychological facts
as such is therefore an illusion.

But not less misleading is the fear that the
system of physiological psychology may interfere with the values of our practical life.   It
stands and falls with the conviction that the psychical facts which are conceived as dependent
upon the brain machinery are the real inner
experience which embraces our duties and responsibilities.   A philosophical inquiry into the

relations of psychology to reality cannot leave any doubt that such a belief is untenable. In our real life our objects of action are not ideas which are separated from the physical things, but the physical and psychical objects form one undifferentiated object of will, which from merely secondary logical motives is divided into a physical and psychical part, and is then conceived as independent of the acts of the subject. And these acts themselves are also never given to us as contents of consciousness, never as objects, but as functions which we feel and live through. Objects and subjective acts are thus alike transformed into something which they never are in reality as soon as the objects are conceived as severed from the will and differentiated into physical and psychical parts and the subjective acts are conceived as psychical objects. All this psychology must do in the interest of special logical purposes of which we shall examine later some of the motives and some of the consequences. But whatever the motives may be, it is clear that this construction of psychical objects, which precedes all special psychological work, excludes from the start the possibility that any connection and relation into which these psychical facts enter can decide about the relations and connections of the real life.

There is thus no emotional interest involved in the question whether a smaller or a larger part of the psychical facts must be conceived as the accompaniment of brain functions; the problem is merely logical and theoretical, as are also the considerations which lead to the ultimate answer of the question. It is true that the naturalists and psychologists themselves are mostly inclined, in the eagerness of their specialistic work, to overlook and to ignore this logical basis of the relations, and to be satisfied with a merely empirical foundation. The relation between mind and brain seems to them a fact of observation, a chance fact whose limits must be found by careful inquiry of the verifiable occurrences. They are not conscious of the deeper spring of this inquiry; they follow their scientific instinct as discoverers, and do not feel that this instinct is controlled by logical demands which decide what in the realm of observation ought to be acknowledged as fact, and what ought to be transformed till it satisfies the theoretical postulates.

II

Of course even the layman is familiar with plenty of instances in which the empirical facts suggest the view that the psychical facts somehow depend upon the brain. Popularly best known are the abnormal processes. A man becomes blind or deaf if special parts of the brain are destroyed by a hemorrhage; his intelligence

becomes disintegrated if he suffers from para-
lysis of the brain ; the brain state of sleep brings
with it the psychical wonders of dreams ; a blow
on the head may induce a state of fainting in
which all mental life disappears ; and chemical
substances introduced into the blood circulation
of the brain change our moods and emotions.
Such generally known experiences are supplemented by more complicated facts from all quarters. The mental life of animals shows itself
to be parallel in its development to the differentiation of the central nervous system ; the facul-
ties of human individuals appear to correspond
to a full development of the brain, the mental
life of the idiot to belong to a brain of inhibited
growth. To this class of facts belong all the
experiments of the physiologist who shows that
the artificial extirpation of a special centre in
the hemispheres of the brain destroys the peripheral function, a function which, on the other
hand, can be artificially produced by an electrical
stimulation of the intact centre. Here belong
also the observations of comparative anatomy,
which prove the development of special brain
parts to be increased or decreased in different
animal groups according to the higher or lower
state of special psychical functions ; for instance,
the high development of the olfactory lobe in
animals which have a fine sense of smell. The
most different methods here work together to

make the collection of a large number of detailed facts possible, and yet the psychologist follows a wrong track if he believes that the results which are yielded by such methods must be decisive for his psychophysical convictions.

If the question were really a merely empirical one, we should be obliged to limit the extension of the psychophysical parallelism to the few psychological processes for which the natural sciences have already found the physiological substratum, but in that moment all the interest of the psychologist would disappear. He acknowledges, in response to a logical demand, that every single psychical fact has its physiological counterpart or the whole inquiry becomes a useless and time-wasting luxury. Whether the psychophysical connections have one exception or a million is indifferent; the belief that the connection exists without exception is the chain on which the whole pyschophysical system hangs, and it must fall if the chain is broken, whether broken once or a thousand times. If it were otherwise — that is, if the psychophysical connections were merely results of empirical observation — they would form an appendix to scientific psychology which would be at least unnecessary for the real psychological work. Psychology describes and explains the psychological facts; it is therefore not its task to study anything which lies outside of the field of psychical facts, if such extension to the non-psychical facts is not logically necessary for the study of the psychical facts themselves. The study of the connections between mind and body would then stand as a special empirical science between psychology and physics, but it would not be a part of psychology itself. Such, however, is not the case. Psychology needs the psychophysical connection for its own special work, needs it as a logical supposition without which it cannot fulfill its proper task, and it therefore acknowledges the completeness of the connection independent of the special empirical observations. Psychophysical parallelism brings with it no ethical danger and no materialistic consequences, because the connected objects do not belong to reality, and are merely theoretical constructions for special logical purposes; but in these constructed systems the connection is absolutely complete and exceptionless or it is altogether useless for psychology. The decoration of our psychological lecture courses with pretty physiological bric-a-brac and the trimming up of our text-books with physiological wood-cuts can hardly be admitted as an end in itself.

Why does the psychologist transcend the limits of the psychical world and look over into the physical world, which is, as the name indicates, never the direct object of his interests? The usual answer is that the psychical facts need the

physical substratum for their explanation ; but I
think we can go a long step farther and say that
even the description of the psychical facts needs
and constantly presupposes the reference to the
physical world, and that it is therefore an illusion
to believe that psychology can fulfill at least the
first part of its work, the description of its
material, without transgressing the boundaries
of consciousness.

III

Description means the communication of an
object by the communication of its elements.
Other ways of communication are open, but
only that method which analyzes the object into
elements and fixates the elements for the purpose of communication is a description. The
choice of the elements and their fixation also can
of course reach very different levels. We may
analyze an animal by separating the chief parts
which we perceive from the outside, or we may
tear it in pieces to find out the inner parts also ;
we may make a careful anatomical dissection
which separates the different tissues, or we may
advance to a histological analysis which discrimi-
nates the different microscopical cells. The description thus stands the higher the more our
choice of elements takes account of the causal
connections, but even the most popular and unscientific report describes on the basis of an ana-

lysis. In the same way the fixation of the elements to be communicated may be increasingly accurate: we may be satisfied to describe the color or the form of the parts of the animal by using the names of general conceptions which include many similar objects, calling it green or oval, or we may advance to a determination of the number of ether vibrations and make measurement of the dimensions in thousandths of a millimeter: the principle remains the same.

How far can we describe psychological objects in the same way, — an idea, for instance? A corresponding analysis is certainly possible. We cannot really isolate the psychical elements, but we can certainly separate them in consciousness, turning the attention to one element after the other, in our self-observation. Here also many stages are possible; the highest stage, corresponding to the microscopical analysis of the anatomist, is reached by self-observation under the experimental conditions which our laboratories furnish, — in other words, the analysis may approach more and more nearly those elements which are the necessary footholds for the explanation of the facts; but in any case there is no theoretical objection to the analysis of mental facts. Quite different is the second factor of the descriptive process, the fixation of these elements for the purpose of communication. We can say without limitation: a psychical element can never be directly communicated, because communication presupposes the possibility of a mutual sharing in the object of experience, while the psychical objects are from their nature strictly individual property.

If we communicate by other methods than description, for instance by suggestion or gestures, the other person takes part in our intentions and purposes, and these intentions are then the object of the communication. But these intentions are not themselves psychical objects; they are the ideal points towards which the meaning of our ideas is directed, and the intention towards which my ideas point may very well be at the same time the goal for the attitudes of the other. But we ask whether the content of consciousness itself can possibly be an object in which the other can take part, and this alone we deny. What my ideas mean and intend is something in which any other may participate, but my ideas themselves belong to me alone, and can, as psychical objects, never be the ideas of any one else. My consciousness is my castle, and even if a mind-reader finds out my most hidden thoughts, his claim does not mean that he has caught a glimpse within my castle walls. He does not become conscious of my psychical contents, but he produces in himself ideas which he claims correspond to my ideas; but not the slightest sensation can ever belong to his and to my consciousness together. All this is not a matter of chance; we cannot think of any psychical fact for which it could be otherwise. In reality the physical thing and our idea of it are one object, and as soon as we differentiate it into a physical and psychical part we have no other principle of division than this one, that we call physical whatever is the possible object of experience for several subjects, and psychical whatever cannot be experienced by more than one. All the other differences are secondary consequences of this fundamental principle, and we have thus no reason to be surprised that we find the latter true without exception. No molecule moves in the world which cannot be an object for every one, and no sensation arises in a consciousness which can be shared with a second subject.

The difference in the communication of physical and psychical objects is now evident. However I may analyze the physical thing, each element is an object for me and my neighbor at the same time, my object becomes his object too, he can see it, touch it, hear it like myself, and my communication is thus a demonstration which fulfills its logical purpose in the most ideal way, and my words have merely the function of directing attention to the common property. But it is not necessary that the physical object should be present to our senses; the words will fulfill their communicating purpose no less if they refer to an object which was experienced in earlier time, or if the objects themselves were never given; at least their elements may have been shared. Whatever the form of the communication about the physical world may be, this reference to the physical world as the object of common experience is always given. If I say it rains, the other may never have seen rain, but by the conceptions of water, sky, globule, falling and so forth I can describe the rain from its elements, and each of these factors is understood through its relation to the objective world. And if even these conceptions were unknown, they could finally be described by the mere measurements in space and time, the knowledge of which is presupposed in the acknowledgment of other subjects.

There is no one of those who perceive the outer world to whom I cannot describe the rain and the snow and the thunder in terms of their elements; but how different if I wish to communicate that I am sorry, or glad, or afraid. In practical life the words "I am afraid" do not appear less descriptive than the words "it rains," and yet they have a quite different basis. Not the least element in my fear as psychical content can be demonstrated and offered for participation to others. Whether they call fear a state which I call joy or violet odor no direct description can decide. However I may analyze it the elements of my fear are just as incommunicable as is the emotion as a whole.

But psychical states must be described somehow; otherwise the possibility of psychology would be excluded. If they are not directly communicable we must take refuge in indirect methods; if the psychical facts are never object for two, and thus strictly individual, we must link them with physical processes which belong to all. We understand what we mean by the words fear, or shock, or joy, because we have learned to use the words for those mental states which are connected with special physical occurrences. The physical objects with which we link them may be foregoing causes or following effects; in any case we have an outer foothold for them. We may call shock the mental state which follows a sudden strong stimulus, or the mental state which precedes a sudden contraction of the muscles; either way is sufficient to separate the one state from others for the purposes of practical life. But it is clear that this method also is not only dependent upon the merely empirically founded belief that the same causes or effects are connected with the same psychical processes, but above all that it is not a description, because the constitution and the elements of the state are not communicated at all. Is there no case in which the logical demands are better fulfilled?

This is now clearly the fact as regards the ideas. The emotions link themselves with physical causes or effects, and everything in respect to them is dependent upon doubtful observations and interpretations; the ideas, on the other hand, stand in a relation to physical things which is anchored in philosophical ground and independent of chance observation; the ideas mean things, and the physical things and the ideas by which we mean them are in reality one and the same object. Here we have a logically necessary connection which holds firm for the elements as well as for the whole. The idea means the thing, and any sensation in the idea means a feature of the thing. The tone, the smell, the color as sensation can thus be communicated indirectly by reference to the sounding, smelling, luminous physical object, and any degree of exactness can be reached by the increasingly accurate description of the physical side. The ideas have thus a perfectly exceptional situation. No other mental state can find such logically necessary connection with the physical world, as a feeling or volition or emotion or judgment finds merely empirical connections, and moreover connections only in which the whole refers to a whole physical thing, but not every element to a special feature of the physical object.

Ideas and their elements alone can thus find a logically satisfactory description in psychology;

the description is indirect, but it is at least a communication of elements. And yet it is easy to understand that under one condition this ideal method of description which we find for the ideas may be found at our disposal for all the other mental states as well. Psychology would then be able to offer a complete description of its material. The one condition is this. Let us call the elements into which we can analyze our ideas by means of self-observation by the name sensations. It may then be that all the non-ideational mental states also are made up of sensations. An emotion or volition is never an idea, but their elements may be the same, just as the organic and inorganic substances in nature are composed of the same chemical elements. If an emotion or judgment or volition were a complex of sensations, that is, a complex of possible elements of ideas, then of course we could describe all psychical facts with the same logical completeness and safety, as every element of these subjective states would be exactly determined by reference to that particle of the physical world which is meant by it as soon as it becomes part of an idea; that is, that with which it is identical from the standpoint of undifferentiated reality.

Modern psychology, like every other active and productive science, has had no leisure to stop and inquire for the logical purposes in the service of which its work is done. The scientist

follows his instincts, and these instinctive energies carry him, perhaps, more safely to the goal
than a conscious reflection on his ends and means;
but the philosopher must recognize these under-
lying purposes, and must bring all specialistic
work within this general point of view. If we
take such attitude toward the work in psychology
of the last twenty years, we can easily see that
not the least and not the most unimportant part
of it has been done in the unconscious service
of this one end — to make the non-ideational
states of mind describable. We have seen that
only one possibility would allow that. They are
describable in case they can be considered as
combinations of sensations; our goal is, therefore, to replace the real emotions, judgments,
volitions, and so on, by complexes of sensations.
Complicated transformations are necessary for
this purpose, and yet the psychologist must work
in the belief and with the claim that these sensations are not the result of his transformations,
but that he has discovered in them the real parts
of those mental states.

All the most modern theories which analyze
the emotions into complexes of bodily sensations,
and the will into ideational elements, and seek
sensational substance even in the most subtle
shades of the mind and in the most fugitive feelings, have here their hidden spring. This movement is unlimited; no content of consciousness

can resist its impulse. The aim of the psychologist is to describe the mental facts ; he must, therefore, presuppose that all mental facts are describable, and, since only elements of ideas can be described, that every content of consciousness is in reality a combination of sensations. As long as the substitution remains incomplete the psychologist feels that he has not discovered the true nature of the facts. The belief that we connect mental with physical processes merely in the service of explanation is thus an illusion ; the simplest description demands just the same.

IV

These claims of description do not mean that the demand for explanation does not introduce any new features into the system of relations between the physical and the psychical worlds. We can say even that a connection of a quite different character must be acknowledged as soon as we try to understand every psychical phenomenon from its foregoing causes. This new and in many ways higher form of psychophysical connection also can be developed here only in general terms. In this case also the principle itself may be more or less masked in the soul of the psychologist who uses it, and here again everything depends upon logical demands which do not allow an exception, and not upon empirical observation.

We may start from the empirical claim that
all our mental life goes on in our organism; this
means at the outset only that my ideas and feelings are with me now in this town, in this room,
in this body, probably in this head, but it does
not include any hypothesis as to the relation of
mind and body.   My mental states are not outside of my epidermis, but they may go on some-
where, for instance at a special point of my brain,
absolutely independent of the functions of the
organism.   Of course this empirical starting
point is itself reached only by a complicated
remodeling of the reality.   Primarily the inner
experience has no spatial quality at all, and is
thus neither in a room nor in a brain; space is a
form of its objects, not a form of its own reality.
But this introjection of the mental facts into the
physical organism may be acknowledged here as
granted without a discussion of the different
steps which lead to it.   Even when this point is
reached, however, many possibilities of interpretation are open; it is only the goal that lies
clear before us: we must explain the psychical
facts.

The wish to explain the psychical facts is not
an accidental afterthought resulting from an
abundance of curiosity; rather it is this wish
which has created the psychological facts as
such.   In reality our objects are objects for the
will, that is, values.   In striving towards the ful-

fillment of the duties which life brings to us we have an interest in determining what we have to expect from the objects in so far as they are independent of our will. We thus separate the object from the real active subject for the one purpose of determining our justified expectations in regard to the changes of the objects. In doing so we create in thought independent objects, which we call physical in so far as they are objects for every subject, and psychical in so far as they are objects for one subject only. The world is thus re-thought as physical and psychical phenomena only under the pressure of the intention to find out the influence which the object will have on the future, that is, the effects which it will produce. In other words, we acknowledge psychical objects as such merely as factors in a system of causes and effects, that is, as factors in an explainable system. We cannot ask whether the psychical and physical facts are explainable or not; the possibility of their explanation is their only legitimate claim to existence. If we wish to take another attitude toward the experience, — the attitude of appreciation and inner understanding, for instance, — then we deal with the inner life as it is given in reality, and nothing suggests that transformation which creates psychical and physical objects.

How is the explanation of psychical phenomena possible? We consider a phenomenon

explained as soon as we can show that it is
necessarily connected with another existing fact
which precedes. At the first glance this demand seems to be satisfied whenever we can
bring two facts under an empirical law which
says whenever A occurs B must follow. The
necessity of the connection between the single
facts appears then as a logical consequence of
the general fact which the law reports ; it must
be so and not otherwise this time because it is always so. Psychology and physics therefore seek
empirical laws. The attraction of the iron is
explained by the laws of electricity, and the reproduction of the idea is explained by the laws
of association. The two sciences seem in this
respect perfectly parallel, and yet they mean
something theoretically absolutely different. All
the laws of the physical universe are in the last
analysis applications of the laws of mechanics.
The question is not whether every empirical law
is already recognized in its mechanical factors,
but it must be acknowledged that natural science
has not reached its ideal end till the physical
world is understood as a world of atoms which
move according to mechanical laws. All physical, chemical, and biological laws are then merely
applications and combinations of the mechanical
laws for special complexes of atoms.

None of the empirical laws are as such necessary connections for our intellect ; they are con-

densed experiences, and if the experiences were otherwise the laws would be changed. The mechanical axioms, on the other hand, are of a very different character ; they are the necessary forms of our apperception of the outer world, — the forms of connection which make the thinking of a connected world of objects possible at all, — and the aim to transform all empirical laws ultimately into mechanical ones is thus the unavoidable consequence of the logical nature of the latter. The mechanical laws are therefore the real basis of all necessity in the physical connections. The physical or chemical or biological laws would in themselves not contain anything which could convince us that an event must happen just so and not otherwise, but as soon as we understand them to be complications of mechanical laws they are logically indispensable. All our trust in the necessity of the physical laws is thus based finally on the conviction, that if we knew all we should recognize every law as a consequence of the mechanical axioms which are laws of thought applied to the conception of space and time.

All the axiomatic doctrines about causal connections in the universe depend upon one law, which is the fundamental presupposition for the existence of the physical world, the law that the causes and effects are quantitatively equal. The totality of physical processes can then be expressed in causal equations, and every effect can theoretically be determined and exactly calculated from the causes. As all physical laws can thus be reduced to mechanical axioms, which are ultimately dependent upon this postulate of causal equations, the necessity of the physical universe finds here its real foundation; this ultimate axiom links all physical processes in the world by the chain of necessity, and thus admits, theoretically, an absolutely perfect explanation.

Nothing of this kind is possible, on the other hand, for the empirical laws of the psychical world. The laws of association and all the other empirical laws, in which modern psychology condenses the results of observation, can never be transformed into causal equations, and therefore never based on a foundation of necessity. They can never make us understand that with a special preceding cause absolutely this special effect must result. Why is it so? Why is all that gives its ultimate meaning and strength to physical law definitively denied to the psychical laws? It is not a matter of chance; no, it is the result of the fundamental act by which the subject divides the real object into a physical and a psychical thing, meaning by physical all that is a possible object for every subject, by psychical all that is a possible object for one subject only. This definition makes it

logically necessary that the physical object shall
not disappear and shall not be newly created,
but must be equal in all changes, while the psychical object, which cannot be the object of two
subjective acts, must therefore be created and
disappear in every new act. One psychical object can then not contain another, and can hence
not be considered as its multiple. It cannot be
understood, therefore, as a measurable quantity,
and is thus eternally unfit for a causal equation,
and therefore for a connection by necessity.

The claim that psychological facts as such can
never be directly connected by necessity may be
misunderstood as meaning that the acts which
form our inner life have no inner connection.
The opposite is true. Our inner life in its real
activity is bound together in all its acts, but it is
an inner connection, not an outer one, as it refers
to the will, while objects can have no other connection than a causal one. The real acts of our
life bind each other teleologically by their intentions and meanings, but as soon as we transform
the acts into psychical objects this inner connection loses all its meaning. Our acknowledgment
of premises binds us in acknowledging the conclusions, but this connection of judgments is
only logically, that is, teleologically, necessary ;
psychologically the judgments as psychical contents can connect themselves with a wrong conclusion just as well as with the logical one.

The connection of our real inner life is not a causal one, while psychological facts as such, that is, as objects, find causal connection or are not connected at all. We have seen that they cannot necessarily be connected in a direct way, because they cannot enter into a causal equation. To concede that they ought then not to be explained at all is still less possible, as we have seen that we conceive mental life as a series of psychical objects merely for the purpose of linking it causally. It follows that we must then take the way which we were forced to choose in the interest of description; that is, we must try to do indirectly what is impossible by direct methods, we must connect the unexplainable psychical world with the explainable physical world. If the idea of the physical world includes the postulate that every physical process can be understood as the necessary result of the foregoing process, and if we are able to show for every psychical process that it is connected with a physical one, we can consider the psychical facts themselves as causally connected whenever the corresponding physical processes are causally linked.

V

The purpose of this connection would be fulfilled by any material that shows a logically constant relation. In the discussion of the

principles of description we have seen that only
one connection between psychical and physical
facts — that between perception and perceived
object — has logical necessity, because this connection can be deduced from primary identity.
It is evident that this relation cannot be used, at
'least in this direct form, for the purposes of explanation. By description we aim at making the
described mental state a kind of public property;
every one who understands the description finds
the idea which suits the description in his own
mind; and we must therefore link it with a part
of the physical world, which is practically at the
disposal of every one. The explanation, on the
other hand, does not seek to formulate a proposition about the mental states of other subjects;
it strives to set forth the one mental fact which
actually appears in me or in you. It must thus
refer to a part of the physical world which belongs to the individual, that is, to our body.
Our body is, of course, also like every physical
thing, an object of perception for all, and just
for that reason it is possible to take the processes
in the body on which the explanation is based as
material for description and communication; but
in a more essential sense my body is an individual object, as it is the one object whose local
and temporal relations to other objects determine
my individual view of the world. If we describe
an idea the reference to such a practically indi-

vidual object would be unsatisfactory, as it must be linked with the corresponding idea in every one to be a real description. If we explain an idea the reference to a practically common object would be useless, as we are seeking to explain a strictly individual fact, the psychical object which I have in this special moment. In the description of the idea of the moon I refer to the moon itself, claiming that wherever the physical moon exists there is given the material from which can be learned what idea I mean. But if I wish to explain why I now have the perception of the moon it would not do to refer again merely to the existence of the moon, since the fact that the moon exists certainly does not logically imply that every one at present has the perception of the moon in consciousness. It is logically necessary that whenever, for the purpose of explanation, psychical facts are linked with physical ones the physical processes must be processes in the individual bodies. We can even add that it must be a process in the body which cannot be an object for our neighbors in the same way as for ourselves. A process of my peripheral organs would thus be as unsatisfactory a means of explanation as the existence of the moon. The fact that something happens to my hand, for instance, cannot serve as explanation for the appearance of a special mental state, for then my neighbor, who can perceive my hand as I do, would necessarily have the same feeling if that hand process and the feeling were two objects which really belonged together.   A central part of the body, which cannot be the object of sense perception while it is part of my body, is alone in question.   This is the reason that all the peripheral parts of the body can be and always are material for our descriptions, for instance in the reference to muscles, joints, glands, and so on, while the brain, which is not an object of perception, can never be used for the description.   Exactly the opposite is necessarily true of the explanation.

We thus need for explanation a process in the physical individual body which is not a possible object of perception while we have the psychical experience, and for which can be found a univocal and necessary connection with the psychical object.   This condition is realized for the perceptive idea and that brain process which stands in causally necessary dependence upon the perceived object.   The relation between the perceptive idea, on the one side, and the brain process which is produced by the perceived object on the other side, fulfills those necessary conditions in ideal completeness, inasmuch as the connection between the idea and its object is based on epistemological identity and the relation between the object and its effect on the individual brain is necessary from physical caus-

ality. The brain stimulation which is caused
by the moon is then not conceived as a cause
for the perception of the moon any more than
the perceived object itself was conceived as the
cause. The moon is the cause of the brain
action, but not of the idea. The material moon
belongs to the perception of it primarily, not as
a cause, but as the counterpart which is in epistemological reality identical with the perceptive
idea; and it is merely this logical relation that
is kept up when the physiological effect of the
moon in our brain is substituted for the moon
itself. This brain excitement, also, is then in
no way the cause of the idea and the idea in
no way the effect of the brain action; even the
usual metaphors which say that it is the inside
of the brain process, or that it is parallel to the
brain process, or that they belong together as
do a concave and a convex surface, are merely
practically useful expressions for a relation of a
strictly logical character which is derived from
epistemological identity. The psychophysical
parallelism of brain function and idea does not,
therefore, seek at all to explain the idea by the
physiological process, or vice versa, but merely
to state that they necessarily belong together,
and thus to admit the further consequence that
whenever the physical process is causally produced the parallel psychical idea must be
conceived as existing. Causality thus connects

only the physical objects directly, while the psychical ideas are indirectly linked as accompaniments of the physiological processes. We have seen that such a physical causal connection is in principle a connection of absolute necessity, not comparable with the combination suggested by an observed regularity. So far, then, as the ideas can be understood as counterparts of physiological processes which are causally connected, this convincing necessity binds them, while as merely psychical facts they were disconnected members.

If it were our goal to extend this method of indirect causal binding to the whole content of consciousness, three conditions would have to be fulfilled. First, the psychophysical parallelism which expresses the relation of the brain process to the idea would have to be acknowledged for the parts of the idea also; every element of the idea would have to correspond to a special part of the physiological process which the idea as a whole accompanies. Secondly, every content of consciousness must be capable of analysis into possible elements of ideas, that is, into sensations; and thirdly, the physiological processes, which are conceived as accompaniments of all contents of consciousness, must be capable of being linked by physical causality, either among themselves or with the events of the universe outside of the brain. Of these three conditions

we have seen the second one to be fulfilled in so
far as we acknowledge the mental life to be describable.   The transformation of the inner life
into sensations was the only way to describe it,
and as the possibility of description is granted as
a presupposition of psychology, therefore we have
a right to presuppose that all mental states are
complexes of sensations, however far we may be
at present from a full knowledge of all the elements which compose it.   The fulfillment of the
first and third conditions can, of course, be given
merely by the work of the physiologist; the
psychologist can hardly add anything.   The
physiologist, on the other hand, cannot find any
insurmountable difficulty in striving towards a
demonstration of their possibility.   The overwhelming manifoldness of the histological elements of the central nervous system and the
complication of its structure, the difficulty of
observing its functions in a direct way, and
many other peculiar factors open an almost unlimited field to the interpretation of the physiologist; there is no reason why he could not select
as truth merely those facts which point towards
the fulfillment of the two mentioned conditions,
and why he could not supplement these facts by
constructions which make up a system in which
these logical presuppositions for the explicability
of the psychical facts are fulfilled.   Exactly this
and nothing else the modern brain physiologist

is attempting, and, like all other scientists, he must presuppose that the goal at which he is aiming can be reached. He thus takes for granted that every sensation is accompanied by a special brain process, and that all brain processes can be explained through physical causality.

Under these circumstances the totality of our mental life can be conceived as linked indirectly by real necessity, but it is not less clear that under these circumstances our interest as psychologists is directed merely to the general theory of psychophysical parallelism and not to the special facts of the psychophysical connections. We must acknowledge that every mental fact is the accompaniment of a special brain process, and this absolutely without any possible exception, because under this condition alone is it possible to conceive the psychical objects as causally connected, and it was for the purpose of causal interpretation only that the transformation of the inner experience into psychical objects was made. But we cannot have as psychologists any interest in the question of the special brain process which accompanies a special given psychical phenomenon; that is physiology, and psychology has nothing to learn from it. We take for granted that such a connection exists, indeed our whole explanatory psychology would collapse if we allowed the slightest exception; but we do not

learn anything about the psychical facts themselves when we hear that the process takes place
in the cortex or in the subcortical centres, in the
ganglion cell or in the dendrite, or in the front
part or in the side part of the brain.   Moreover,
it is now clear why the conviction of the psychologist, that every mental state has its physiological accompaniment, is fully independent of
the special discoveries of physiology and pathology; it is not the result of observations, but of
postulates which are logically unavoidable if we
are to have psychology at all.

VI

There remains, of course, the possibility of the
objection that the empirical facts do not allow a
construction which satisfies such psychophysical
postulates, and that therefore the hypothetically
demanded psychology is an end which can never
be reached, and thus an impossible science.   If
such view is correct, if a consistent descriptive
and causally explaining psychology cannot be
realized, it is evident whither the inheritance
must go.   If the mental life cannot be explained
causally, — and that means psychophysically, —
then the whole inner experience must be given
over to the subjectifying sciences, which interpret it by its meaning and by its values, taking
the inner life as a unity and as a will act, which
it certainly is in reality.   The objections to ex-

plaining psychology from this side are essentially two. On the one side, it is said that
the physiological system, which alone carries the
responsibility for all psychological connections,
can never explain the intellectual and teleological
character of our connections in consciousness.
On the other hand, it is emphasized that the structure and the connections of the brain are totally
inadequate to satisfy the other demand that a
special brain process shall correspond to every
possible variation of the psychical experience.
These two objections must now engage our attention.

It is quite true that the first claim seems antagonistic to all the instinctive feelings of a
popular philosophy. The psychophysical parallelism which we have deduced as a necessary
logical postulate if psychology is to exist at all,
demands indeed not less than the determination
of all our psychophysical functions by the dispositions and causal connections of processes in
physical matter. Whatever we think, feel, will,
and act can, as psychophysical process, be exactly
determined by the totality of active and latent
causes in the physical system. This seems to deprive our inner life of all its values, and, as we
are accustomed to connect every appreciation in
life with inner experience, it seems deplorable
to conceive this inner life as dependent upon the
blind movements of feelingless matter. But we

have emphasized from the beginning that here
every emotional interference means confusion.
Values and duties, freedom and responsibility,
belong to the inner life in its real activity, but
not to the system of psychological facts into
which we have transformed the inner experience.
As soon as the remoulding of the reality into
physical and psychical objects is completed the
latter do not stand nearer to the attitudes of the
real personality than do the former. Whether
a result is produced by the causal mechanism of a
physical substance, or by the causal actions of
a mental stuff, is not different from the point
of view of dignity ; both schemes are equally far
from the teleological actions of the real subject.
The question is thus merely whether the state of
science makes it appear possible to explain the
totality of psychophysical functions, even the
wisest word and the best deed, as the necessary
product of physiological processes.

The problem is a biological one, and the biologist need not wait for the philosopher with his
epistemological postulates deduced from the necessary limitations of psychology. The biologist
finds a direct impulse to such considerations independent of all psychological questions in the
fundamental principle of physics, the law of the
conservation of energy. He is, of course, mistaken in believing that it is based less on philosophical reasons than on empirical observation,

but it is in any case a non-psychological principle which leads to the same result as the psychological discussions: every action, every expression, every function which seems to refer to psychical experience must find the totality of its causes on the physical side, since every exception would be a physical miracle. The slightest physical action which is not completely determined by the foregoing physical causes would represent an increase of the sum of energy, a concession by which the whole system of physical science would be hopelessly undermined, and which must be uncompromisingly denied, even at the present stage of science, which is certainly still far from demonstrating the constancy of the sum of energies in all variations. Thus the difference between the two possible ways of the biologist is merely this: When he starts from the physical laws he seeks to explain human actions, and this demand for physical explanation of the motor discharges leads him to the conviction that the psychical states also are, from his standpoint, merely accompaniments of physiological processes. When he starts from the psychical facts and their unfitness for causal interdependence, he aims directly at finding a physiological accompaniment to every psychical fact, and thence comes to the conclusion that the motor discharges can be explained through these accompanying brain excitements; the final outcome, however, is in both cases the same.

Does the biologist ever feel discouraged in such studies by the valuable character of the processes, by that factor which seems to naïve eclecticism not only the moral hindrance, but also the chief theoretical difficulty? Does it retard his explanations when the result of the brain functions shows logical and practical adjustment to the outer conditions and to the interests of the acting organism, just as if a deliberating intelligence had opened and closed the right switches and tracks in the cerebral system? Decidedly not; more than that, we may say that this wisdom and usefulness is for him the key to the whole situation.

The biologist naturally compares the postulated functions of the brain with the actions of the other organs in the organism and finds everywhere the same adaptation and the same selectiveness without ever taking refuge in the too easy hypothesis that an intellectual subject stands behind the stage and pulls the wires. Such a soul hypothesis is no doubt convenient, but it leaves all the problems unsolved, and would be in itself a still more complicated system to explain. After a hearty meal millions and millions of cells are working in our vegetative system which coöperate in the interest of the nutrition of the organism with a wisdom no council of chemists could surpass; yet the physiologist would think it a cheap hypothesis to suppose that a stomach-soul controls these useful and adapted actions.   The same thing is true of the apparatus of blood circulation, of breathing, of procreation, and so on.   But everywhere the biologist takes this usefulness not as increasing the difficulty of his explanations, but as the bridge towards a causal understanding; the modern biologist would feel himself lost only on finding a useless or disadvantageous organ which could not be understood as an abnormal individual disturbance, or as the remainder of a formerly useful organ.   The useful organ alone can have found the conditions for its development in the growth of the race.   The digestive apparatus of man with its fairy-tale-like complication can be followed in this phylogenetic development from the highest mammals down to the protozoöns, where the assimilation of nourishing substance is the function of the whole protoplasmic substance.   With the growing differentiation of the organism only those variations of the vegetative apparatus were not eliminated which served the purposes of the organism and its descendants; every useless formation was destroyed in the struggle for existence, and thus lost its chance of being inherited.   It is thus just the useful complications which become explicable on mechanical principles to the biologist of the Darwinian age.

VII

Why not apply this same view to the functions of the brain? One thing is of course evident from the first: the biologist must consider not merely a part of the apparatus, but the whole, as only the whole can be useful. No biology can explain the development of the heart without the peripheral blood vessels, or the liver without the stomach; the brain alone is not the whole, it is the central part, as is the heart in the blood system. The brain is useful merely as the central organ of a system which begins with the sense organs, connects them by a hundred thousand sensory nerves with the central nervous system, and connects this central part, by means of the motor nerves, with the muscles of the organism. The psychophysical functions without muscles to express them, or the centrally controlled motor system without sense-organs to adjust the functions to the outer world, would be biologically useless. This whole arc, from the sense organs through the brain to the muscles, is on the other hand an apparatus not more and not less useful than the circulatory or respiratory apparatus; they all represent a perfect adaptation of the organism to the outer world.

If this arc is looked on as one apparatus, we have indeed no difficulty in following the phylogenetic development downward to the lowest

forms in which the functions of this arc were
secured by the protoplasmatic activity of the
whole organism.   Among the protozoöns we find
two types of reaction to outer stimuli : the contraction of the whole body under disadvantageous
stimulation and the pseudopodic extension under
favorable stimulation.   Both reactions are most
useful characteristics, since contraction brings
the smallest possible surface in contact with the
dangerous substance, while extension offers the
largest possible surface to the beneficial sur-
roundings.   It states the problem wrongly to
ask how the lowest animals came to this acquisi-
tion : it is just by virtue of this variation that
the protoplasmic substance becomes an animal.
As soon as organisms with the power of such
reaction exist, the differentiation of the under-
lying substratum of this function is a necessary
accompaniment to the increasing complication
and growth of the animals.   Firstly, the animal
cannot reach its prey and cannot protect itself
against its dangers if at the higher stages of
development the whole body still goes through
the reactions.   The stimulation and the motor
response must become more and more localized
and the transformation of excitement into discharge must thus find isolated paths; we call
them nerves.   But the protective function of
this apparatus still remains too limited for a
higher stage if the reaction answers merely the

outer stimuli of the moment. It needs thus secondly the development of an organ by which the reaction can become the discharge of all the foregoing stimuli together, an organ in which the after effects of earlier impressions remain as molecular dispositions which have a reënforcing or varying or inhibitory influence on the discharges of the new impressions. Such an organ must develop its possibilities steadily in the phylogenetic development as it adjusts the movements of the organism to a circle of conditions which is the wider the more this apparatus is differentiated; we call it the central nervous system. Its biological functions are those which we refer in psychological interpretation to memory, attention, volition, and so forth. In principle it is nothing new; the bug, the frog, the dog, adjust their useful and protective reactions merely to an increasingly large set of stimuli, spread over space and time, while the central nervous system of even the mammal does not produce any movement which better adjusts the organism of its owner to its surrounding than does the protoplastic substance of the infusoria.

Nothing new is brought by the step forwards from animal to man ; it is the steady development of a biological mechanism which does not change its functions in spite of new and characteristic complications. The life of man brings two factors into the evolution which were not unknown but insignificant in lower stages of the living world: the tool and the division of labor. Superficial biologists sometimes believe themselves to be true Darwinians only when they predict for man a development towards an over-man with a still more developed body, and they even go so far as to construct an ethics which shall serve such biological progress. That the biological development cannot suddenly stop is of course true. A higher organism is indeed to succeed the lower one in the human race too, but the development has reached with man a form in which progress does not mean simply differentiation of the body. The tools of technique and the means of communication through which division of labor is possible, in short, the products of civilization, are the new organs of man, and their development in the struggle for existence continues in a direct biological line the progress of the animals. The only biologically possible over-man is the man with higher civilization, and it would correspond to zoölogical laws that he is not more highly developed in his bodily apparatus; the latter may even be reduced, since the man does not need strong legs if he has locomotives, nor strong fists if he has cannons, nor strong eyes if he has microscopes, nor a strong memory if he has libraries.

The tool in its widest sense was indeed the

greatest step forwards, as it means an extension
of the physiological arc at both its ends, characterized by the entirely new attribute that it
is detachable and thus not destroyed in the
death of the organism by which it is produced.
The individual can attach to his arc apparatus
the products of all preceding generations, and
thus readjust his purposes with an incomparable
richness of means.   And in the same direction
works the division of labor, the other great
biological scheme which nature has tried with
man.   The functions of the individual sense-
organ-brain-muscle arc are for the complicated
man not sufficient to bring to his brain all the
stimulations which need motor adjustment or to
produce, even with the tools of civilization, all
the reactions which would be nutritious, protective, and creative.   If one acts for the advantage
of others, and they repay it by acting for his
benefit, a mutual adjustment can be reached by
which a much larger amount of advantageous
motor reaction and sensory stimulation can be
secured for the individual.   The necessary supposition is the development of the means of
communication from the simplest language to
the cable and the printing press and the coin,
and the result is the market and the state.

And yet this civilized man with his warships
and newspapers and universities is not better
adapted to his conditions of life than the micro-

scopical rhizopod to its simpler conditions; in both cases nature has produced that development of the reaction apparatus which is in its functioning useful to the organism, and its very usefulness gives us a foothold for explanation. We naturally think here of one side of human life which seems so fully to contradict such a biological construction that the whole theory apparently loses its value. Man is an ethical being, and our morality finds its value just in the fact that we act without reference to our personal advantage. Nature cannot produce according to biological laws an apparatus which possesses normally functions which are useful to other individuals but disadvantageous to the acting organism. Actions in the interest of the offspring form an exception which explains itself and confirms the rule, but the moral action seems indeed inexplicable as long as every action is explained as a biologically necessary reaction of the organism. But we must separate the motives of the ethical action from the action itself; the anticipated idea may be to the advantage of the neighbor only, and yet the action may have effects which are indirectly advantageous to the actor. In our ethical functions we perform reactions which we do not need for ourselves, but just that we are doing all the time in our economical functions also; the shoemaker makes many more shoes than are necessary to protect his foot. In our economical functions we hope and wait for the exchange, in our ethical functions we do not wait for it, but the exchange comes nevertheless, and only because it comes in the long run could nature afford to create this kind of reaction apparatus. To receive all the great advantages which we enjoy when others are good and helpful and generous to us, there is only one way — we must be generous and good and helpful ourselves. If it were otherwise nature would have abolished the luxury of variations in such moral directions. We praise the sacrifice of life as the highest ethical action, and it is indeed clear that here, at least, no exchange is possible, after the action, if we do not admit fame as a substitute. But here ethical appreciation, which considers the motive only and not the effects, does not bind biology. From a biological standpoint the ethical sacrifice of life is not a proof against the principle that every psychophysical action is useful to the actor; it is merely a case of overfunctioning. We have no useful organ in our body which cannot kill us when we overwork it; if we run too fast our heart may kill us. Whenever the useful ethical apparatus functions with an abnormal intensity, life is lost, but that this intensity is really abnormal follows simply from the fact that if the voluntary sacrifice of life were a normal function there would be no next genera-

tion to learn and to imitate that prescription.
In short, the biologist finds no difficulty in bring-
ing the totality of the psychophysical functions
under the biological and therefore ultimately
under the mechanical aspect; that postulate of
psychology is in this respect thus realizable.
That such biological construction does not touch
at all the problems of the real life and of ethics
is a matter of course.

VIII

It may then be granted that the usefulness
and adaptedness of the psychophysical functions
would not contradict the mere mechanical character of the substratum upon whose causal functions we must think the psychical connections
dependent. But we had a second chief objection before us. The structure of the brain seems
far too uniform to furnish a sufficient manifoldness of functions if we really demand a physiological process corresponding to every possible
variation of the content of consciousness. The
mere number of elements cannot be decisive;
if they are all functionally coördinated they can
offer merely the basis for coördinated psychical
functions. If we have psychical functions of
different orders, it would not help us even if we
had some millions more of the uniform elements.
It would be useless to deny that here indeed exists
a great difficulty for our present psychology; the

only question is whether this difficulty really
opposes the demands and suppositions of psychology or whether it means that the usual theories of to-day are inadequate and must be improved.   It seems to me that the latter is the
case, and that hypotheses can be constructed
by which all demands of psychology can be satisfied without the usual sacrifice of consistency.
The situation is the following : —

The whole scheme of the physiologists operates
to-day in a manifoldness of two dimensions: they
conceive the conscious phenomena as dependent
upon brain excitements which can vary firstly
with regard to their localities and secondly with
regard to their quantitative amount.   These two
variations then correspond to the quality of the
mental element and to its intensity.   In the
acoustical centre, for instance, the different pitch
of the tone sensations corresponds to locally
different ganglion cells, the different intensities
of the same tone sensation to the quantity of the
excitement.   Association fibres whose functions
are not directly accompanied by conscious experiences connect these millions of psychophysical
elementary centres in a way which is imagined
on the model of the peripheral nerve.   No serious attempt has been made to transcend this simple scheme.   Certainly recent discussions have
brought many propositions to replace the simple
physiological association fibre which connects the

psychophysical centres by more complicated systems, — theories, for instance, in regard to the opening and closing of the connecting paths or in regard to special association centres or special mediating cell groups, — but these and others stick to the old principle that the final psychophysical process corresponds to the strength and locality of a sensory stimulation or of its equivalent reproduction, whatever may have brought about and combined the excitements.

It is true that it has been sometimes suggested that the same ganglion cell may also go over into qualitatively different states of excitement, and thus allow an unlimited manifoldness of new psychophysical variations. But it is clear that to accept such an hypothesis means to give up all the advantages of brain localization. The complicatedness of the cell would be in itself sufficient to give ground to the idea that its molecules may reach some millions of different local combinations; and if every new combination corresponds to a sensation, all the tones and colors and smells and many other things may go on in one cell. But then it is of course our duty to explain those connections and successions of different states in one cell, and that would lead to conceiving the cell itself as constructed with millions of paths just like a miniature brain ; in short, all the difficulties would be transplanted into the unknown structure of the cell. If we,

on the other hand, do not enter into such spec-
ulations, the acceptance of qualitative changes
in the cell would bring us to the same point
as if we were satisfied to speak of qualitative
changes of the brain in general. It would not
solve the problem but merely ignore it, and
therefore such an additional hypothesis cannot
have weight.

The only theory which brings in a really new
factor is the theory of innervation feelings.
This well-known theory claims that one special
group of conscious facts, namely, the feelings of
effort and impulse, are not sensations and therefore not parallel to the sensory excitements, but are
activities of the consciousness and parallel to the
physiological innervation of a central motor path.
At this point of course comes in at once the
opposition of the philosophical claim that every
psychical fact must be, as we have seen, a content of consciousness, and made up of sensations,
that is, of possible elements of ideas, to become
describable and explainable at all. The so-called
active consciousness, the philosopher must hold,
has nothing to do with an activity of the consciousness itself, as consciousness means from
the psychological standpoint only the kind of
existence of psychical objects. It cannot do
anything, it cannot have different degrees and
functions, it only becomes conscious of its contents, and all variations are variations of the

content, which must be analyzed without remainder into elements which are theoretically coördinated with the elements of ideas, that is, with the
sensations, while consciousness is only the general
condition for their existence. But also the empirical analysis and experiment of the practical
psychologist are in this case in the greatest harmony with such philosophical claims and opposed
to the innervation theory. The psychologist
can show empirically that this so-called feeling
of effort is merely a group of sensations like
other sensations, reproduced joint and muscle
sensations which precede the action and have
the rôle of representing the impulse merely on
account of the fact that their anticipation makes
inhibitory associations still possible. It would
thus from this point of view also be illogical
to think the psychophysical basis of these sensations different in principle from that of other
sensations. If the other sensations are accompaniments of sensory excitements in the brain,
the feelings of impulse cannot claim an exceptional position.

But are quality and intensity really the only
differences between the given sensations? Can
the whole manifoldness of the content of consciousness really be determined by variations in
these two directions only? Certainly not; the
sensations can vary even when quality and intensity remain constant. As an illustration we may

think, for instance, of one variation which is clearly not to be compared with a change in kind and strength of the sensation ; namely, the variation of vividness. Vividness is not identical with intensity ; the vivid impression of a weak sound and the faint impression of a strong sound are in no way interchangeable. If the ticking of the clock in my room becomes less and less vivid for me the more I become absorbed in my work, till it finally disappears, it cannot be compared with the experience which results when the clock to which I give my full attention is carried farther and farther away. The white impression, when it loses vividness, does not become gray and finally black, nor the large size small, nor the hot lukewarm. Vividness is a third dimension in the system of psychical elements, and the psychologist who postulates complete parallelism has the right to demand that the physiologist show the corresponding process. There are other sides of the sensation for which the same is true ; they share with vividness the more subjective character of the variation, as, for instance, the feeling tone of the sensation or its pastness and presentness. Other variations bring such subjective factors into the complexes of sensations without a possibility of understanding them from the combination of different kinds only ; for instance, the subjective shade of ideas we believe or the abstractedness of ideas in logical thoughts. In short, the sensations and their combinations show besides kind, strength, and vividness still other variations which may best be called the values of the sensations and of their complexes. In the interest of simplicity we intentionally neglected these subjective sides of the sensations when we discussed the methods of description ; it is evident that, in connecting the sensation with the physical world for the purposes of description these sides require reference to the physical relation between the perceived object and the organism. Is the typical theory of modern physiological psychology, which, as we have seen, operates merely with the local differences of the cells and the quantitative differences of their excitement, ever able to find physiological variations which correspond to the vividness and to the values of the sensations ?

An examination without prejudice must necessarily deny this question. Here lies the deeper spring for the latent opposition which the psychophysiological claims find in modern psychology. Here are facts, the opponents say, which find no physiological counterpart, and we must therefore acknowledge the existence of psychological processes which have nothing to do with the physiological machinery. The vividness, for instance, is fully explained if we accept the view that the brain determines the kind and strength of the sensation, while a physiologically independent

subject turns the attention more or less to the
sensation. The more this attention acts the more
vivid the sensation; in a similar way the subjective acts would determine the feeling tone of
the sensation by selection or rejection, and so on.
While the usual theory reduces all to the mere
association of locally separated excitements, such
a theory emphasizes the view that the physiologically determined functions must be supplemented by an apperceiving subject which takes
attitudes. We may call one the association
theory, the other the apperception theory. We
have seen that the association theory is insuffi-
cient to solve the whole problem, but it is hardly
necessary to emphasize that the apperception
theory seeks the solution from the start in a
logically impossible direction, and is thus still
more mistaken than the association theory.

The apperception theory, whatever its special
label and make-up may be, does not see that the
renunciation of a physiological basis for every
psychical fact means resigning the causal explanation altogether, since psychical facts as such
cannot be linked directly by causality, and that
resigning the causal aspect means giving up the
only purpose for which the inner life was ever
transformed into psychical facts. If those ap-
perceptive functions are seriously conceived as
without physiological basis, they represent a
manifoldness which can be linked merely by the

teleological categories of the real life, and we
sink back to the subjectifying view which controls the reality of life, but which is in principle
replaced by the objectifying view as soon as a
psychical object is acknowledged as such.   If
the apperception theory, on the other hand,
wants to live up to the demands of psychology,
that is, to give causal explanations, it can do
so only if it replaces the psychical objects by
constructions which are themselves conceived
on the analogy with physical objects.   As soon
as the ideas are pictured like balls which are
pushed and rolled, then of course a kind of
pseudomechanics and pseudocausality is possible
for the psychical facts themselves, but in that
case the whole indirect connection of psychical
facts by means of the brain would be in all
respects a useless theory ; we have then sufficient
direct causality between the ideas themselves.
Its shortcoming is only that the whole system
is built up on a false metaphor which is to be
rejected from the outset because it gives to the
psychical fact that characteristic which by the
fundamental principle of the differentiation of
objects into physical and psychical is necessarily
reserved for the physical objects.

Of course the illogical apperception theory
would not return in psychology in so many
forms, did it not favor the illusion that it is less
opposed than the association theory to the emo-

tional demands of man.   It is the old psycho-
logistic absurdity that any theoretical idea about
psychological objects can touch the subjectifying interests of the real life.   The apperception
theory, which comes home with the news that
there is a corner in the psychical world where
no causal explanation has as yet been found, is
then welcomed as the bringer of happy hopes;
till later advices come we can still feel ourselves
free and dignified.   The philosophical understanding of that which we mean by a psychological truth and by a transformation into psychical objects, a transformation which would be
utterly meaningless if the apperception theory
were correct, is the only scientific way of over-
coming such illusory conflicts.   As soon as this
fundamental misunderstanding about the meaning of psychophysical theories has taken place,
it is quite natural that the most extreme form of
the apperception theory should have the best
popular chances.   It would be represented in
the so-called transmission theory, which considers
the brain as unessential for the causal connections of the psychical facts and acknowledges
its function merely as an organ of transmission,
whose destruction would not hinder the temporal
continuation of the causal connection of psychical objects.   The immortality which the transmission theory seeks to secure to us is thus
the continuous repetition of objects which have

nothing in common with the real experiences of
our inner life, and which cannot claim anything
else than the fact that the psychologist must
construct them for the purpose of transforming
the teleological reality into a causal system.
Needless to say after all these discussions that
this real subjective life cannot possibly be interested in any psychophysiological theory, and
that with the association and apperception and
transmission theories equally it connects not the
slightest emotional value, except those of logical
satisfaction and disappointment. The philosopher
who bases the hope of immortality on a theory
of brain functions and enjoys the facts which
cannot be physiologically explained, stands, it
seems to me, on the same ground with the astronomer who seeks with his telescope for a place
in the universe where no space exists, and where
there would be thus undisturbed room for God
and the eternal bodiless souls.

IX

We do not here enter upon metaphysical questions ; we discuss the empirical brain theory, and
only deny to the apperception theory the claimed
right to recommend itself by illusory metaphysical promises. But does this bankruptcy of all
varieties of apperception theories necessarily
force us back to the association theory? I do
not think so. The demand of the association

theory that every psychosis should be accompanied by a neurosis cannot be given up, but this neurosis may be thought in a richer way than in the scheme of the associationists. It seems to me, indeed, that the physiological theory works to-day with an abstract scheme with which no observation agrees. We do not know of a centripetal stimulation which does not go over into centrifugal impulses. The studies on the tonicity and actions of voluntary muscles, on the changes in glands and blood vessels, on tendon reflex centres, and so on, show how every psychophysical state discharges itself into centrifugal functions. And yet these perceivable peripheral effects are of course merely a small part of the centrifugal impulses which really start from the end stations of the sensory channel, as most of them probably produce only new dispositions in lower motor centres without going directly over into movement, and others may fade away in the unlimited division of the discharge in the ramification of the system. Those milliards of fibres are not merely the wires to pull a few hundred muscles; no, the centrifugal system represents certainly a most complex hierarchy of motor centres too, and the special final muscle impulse is merely the last outcome of a very complex coöperation of very many factors in the centrifugal system. Manifold as the incoming nerve currents must be, the possibilities of centrifugal discharge and the dispositions in the nervous motor system determine the degrees in which the ganglion cells can transform the centripetal into centrifugal stimulation. It is thus not only the foregoing sensory process, but in exactly the same degree also the special situation of the motor system, its openness and closedness, which governs the process in the centre. Whether the special efferent channel is open or plugged implies absolutely different central processes in spite of the same afferent stimulus.

Here we have, then, a new factor on the physiological side, which is ignored in the usual scheme that makes the psychical facts dependent upon the sensory processes only and considers the centrifugal action of the brain as a later effect which begins when the psychophysical function is over. There is no central sensory process which is not the beginning of an action too, and this centrifugal part of the central process necessarily varies the accompanying psychical fact also. As here the action of the centre becomes the essential factor in the psychophysical process, we may call this view an action theory as over against the association and apperception theories of the day. The action theory agrees, then, with associationism in the postulate that there is no psychical variation without variation on the physiological side, and with

apperceptionism in the conviction that the mere
association of sensory brain processes is insuffi-
cient to play the counterpart to such subjective
variations of the psychical facts as vividness and
values of the sensations. It tries to combine
the legitimate points in both views, and claims
that every psychical sensation as element of the
content of consciousness is the accompaniment
of the physical process by which a centripetal
stimulation becomes transformed into a centrifugal impulse.

This central process thus clearly depends upon
four factors : firstly, upon the local situation of
the sensory track ; secondly, upon the quantitative
amount of the incoming current ; thirdly, upon
the local situation of the outgoing discharge ;
and fourthly, upon the quantitative amount of
the discharge. The first two factors are of course
determined by the incoming current, which can
be replaced by an intra-cortical stimulation from
an associated centre, while the last two factors
are determined by the dispositions of the centrifugal system. The association theory, which
considers the first two factors alone, thinks them
parallel to the kind and strength of the sensation. The action theory accepts this interpretation, and adds that the two other factors determine the values and the vividness of the
sensation,—the values parallel to the local situation of the discharge, the vividness to the open-

ness of the centrifugal channel, and thus to the intensity of the discharge.

If the centrifugal discharge is inhibited, the channel closed, then the sensory process goes on as before, but the impression is faint, unperceived, while it may become vivid later as soon as the hindrance to the discharge disappears. The inhibition of ideas, which remains unexplainable to the associationists, would then mean that a special path of discharge is closed, and thus the idea which needs that discharge for its vividness cannot come into existence; the hypnotizer's words, for instance, close such channels. Only discharges, actions, can be antagonistic, and thus under mutual inhibition; ideas in themselves may be logically contradictory, but not psychologically while one action makes the antagonistic action indeed impossible and the inhibition of ideas results merely from the inhibition of discharges. If this view is correct, it is clear that while we strictly deny the existence of special innervation sensations, we can now say that every sensation without exception is physiologically an innervation sensation, as it must have reached some degree of vividness to exist psychologically at all.

With regard to the local situation of the motor discharge, the manifoldness of possibilities is evident. The channels may be closed in one direction but open in others; the actually resulting discharge must be the product of the situation in the whole centrifugal system, with its milliards of ramifications, and the same sensory stimulus may thus under a thousand different conditions produce a thousand different centrifugal waves, all, perhaps, with the same intensity. The vividness would then be always the same, and yet the difference of locality in the discharge must give new features to the psychical element. A few cases as illustrations must be sufficient. We may instance the shades of time-direction; the same idea may have the subjective character of past, present, and future. It corresponds to three types of discharge : the discharge which does not include action on the object any more appears a past; that which produces action as present; that which prepares the action as future. In this group belong also the feeling tones : the pleasurable shade of feeling based on the discharge towards the extensors, the unpleasant feelings based on the innervation of the flexors. Here belong the differences between mere perception and apperception, as in the one case the discharge is determined by the impression alone, in the other case by associations also. Here belong the characteristics of the abstract conception which may be represented by the same sensational qualities which would form a concrete idea and yet has a new subjective tone because the centrifugal discharge is for the concrete idea a specialized impulse, for the conception a general impulse which would suit all objects thought under the conception. Here belongs, also, the feeling of belief which characterizes the judgment ; the judgment differs psychophysically from the mere idea in the fact that the ideas discharge themselves in a new tonicity, a new set of the lower motor centres, creating thus a new disposition for later reactions. To be sure, many of these discharges lead finally to muscle contractions which bring with them centripetal sensations from the joints, the muscles, the tendons, and these muscle and joint sensations themselves then become a part in the idea, for instance, of time, of space, of feeling. But the new part only reinforces the general tone which is given in the general discharge, and gives to it only the exact detail which gets its character just through the blending of these sensations of completed reactions with the accompaniments of the central discharge.

A consistent psychology thus starts with the following principles : It considers all variations of mental life as variations of the content of consciousness, and this content as a complex object, including in this first presupposition a complicated transformation of the real inner life, a transformation by which the subjectifying view of real life is denied for the psychological system. Every content of consciousness is further considered as a complex of sensations, that is, of possible elements of perceptive ideas. Every sensation is considered as having a fourfold manifoldness, varying in kind, in strength, in vividness, and in value. The physiological basis of every sensation and thus of every psychical element is the physical process by which a centripetal stimulation becomes transformed into a centrifugal impulse, the kind depending upon the locality of the centripetal channel, the strength upon the quantity of the stimulus, the value upon the locality of the centrifugal channel, and the vividness upon the quantity of the discharge. Every transformation of the chaos of so-called facts in the direction towards these ends which are determined by epistemology adds something to the system of psychological science.

Also for these ultimate transformations in the service of explanation is valid what we emphasized in regard to description. The scientist must do his work continually with the feeling that he seeks and discovers facts which preceded his seeking and which he merely brings to view. But the philosopher, at least, cannot forget that such is a low conception of truth, and that the work is a transformation of the reality for the fulfillment of our logical ideals which takes place ultimately in the service of our duties. The seeker for truth is not a miner who digs and digs in the clay of reality till he by chance finds a lump of gold with his shovel, gold which has slumbered there for eternities. The seeker for truth creates like the sculptor who takes the valueless clay of reality to transform it under his hands into the precious plastic work which harmonizes with his ideals.

PSYCHOLOGY AND EDUCATION

I

THE defender of idealistic convictions who arms himself with philosophical arguments to fight against materialism finds himself in combat, not with one group alone, but with two — with those who through serious arguments come to anti-idealistic views and with those who adopt idealism without arguments at all. They may favor idealism through sentimentality, or through mysticism, or, the more frequent case, through laziness and mere lack of understanding the arguments of the other side; their view has no solid foundation, no consistency, no power of resistance. With the first group you can argue; with the second group you cannot debate, as you speak a different language and think with a different logic. As soon as the real fight begins, you feel that the coincidence of aims is only a chance result without significance; the help of these friends is only a hindrance and a trouble, and they ought to be sent away, like the women and children of a besieged city before the real bombardment begins.

This old experience came to me with unusual force when a short time ago I expressed my educational convictions, which take the idealistic view of the teacher's work as against the materialistic doctrines of certain psychological schools. I maintained in some magazine articles that the individual teacher cannot make any direct use of physiological and experimental psychology for his teaching methods. Why this view alone lies in the line of idealism we shall see later. My articles were sharply attacked from the other side, as the progress of a discussion demands, and I was ready to go on fighting. But at the same time I was applauded by sympathizers who did not care for my arguments at all, and who hailed my side only because it was much more convenient not to study psychology and education. They cried naïvely: "Of course the man is right; all experimental and physiological psychology is nonsense, and all study of education is superfluous; let the teachers do just as they like; our grandfathers made it just so." From day to day I became more doubtful with which side I disagreed more fully. If I warn education not to make progress in a wrong direction, must I proclaim by that that we ought to go backward? If I denounce a dangerous misuse of experimental psychology, do I thereby attack experimental psychology itself? If I assert that the interest of the teacher ought not

to go in a misleading direction, do I demand by
that that the teacher ought to be dull and without interest? If I regret that something has become the fad of dilettants, do I ask by that that
scholars also ought not to deal with it? and if I
find fault with the recent development of child
study, do I imply by that the belief that we do
not need a modern science of education? As long
as such confusion exists among assenters equally
with dissenters, we do not need so much argu-
mentation as discrimination. We must have
clearness and exact definitions before we decide
about consent or opposition; and it is not sufficient to dissolve the whole interlaced mass of
conceptions like child study, child psychology,
experimental psychology, physiological psychology, educational psychology, education, instruction, school teaching, etc., etc.; but we must
clear up above all the manifoldness of possible
relations between these factors. An unpretend-
ing effort in this direction is the only direct
purpose of the following lines; they try only
to separate clearly the different questions and to
show soberly what some of us want and what we
do not want. I do not fight now; I only peace-
fully draw a map which indicates the different
opposing positions.

We recognize at the first glance that our
whole group of conceptions has two central
points which are logically independent of each

other: the child and psychology. To simplify the matter, we may start with these two ideas only. Psychology is the science which describes and explains mental phenomena, and what a child is we know perhaps better without than with a scholarly definition. Let us only keep in mind that in the happy fields of child study childhood lasts from the cradle to the end of adolescence, usually to the twenty-fifth year. It is clear that even between these two conceptions a number of relations are possible, and the willingness to transform one of these relations in reality does not include the duty to do the same with the others. The child, for instance, can be taught psychology, or it can be taught after the scheme of psychology, or it can be an object of psychology, or it can be an instrument of psychology, and so forth. We can be enthusiastic for the one and nevertheless at the same time detest the other.

The simplest of the cases mentioned is the first: the child may learn psychology. But even here several modifications are possible, as it may be learned at different ages, by different methods, and different parts of psychology may be in question. I for one should say that there is a field here for sound and productive work, and that we should not be hindered and crippled by the lack of experience in this region, or by the pitiable results which have had to be recorded in the past when an antiquated and indigestible psychology was taught by incompetent persons to unwilling pupils, by the driest possible methods. For the instruction in modern empirical psychology, at least in its elements, the high school seems not at all too early a stage; only the work must be fully adapted to the practical experiences of the child, must be richly illustrated by simple experimental demonstrations, and must be given by competent men who could make a whole address out of every sentence they speak. There are few fields where a born teacher can better show his power and his wits. Philosophical psychology, including the historical forms of rational and speculative psychology, — certainly a most important subject for the college student, — like all other real philosophy, decidedly does not belong in the school; the more so as any instruction in philosophy which means more than drill in logic and preaching in ethics can become valuable in any case only if a real scholar, and not a second-hand man, offers it. I should also exclude from the school the relations of psychology to the details of brain physiology and the whole of pathological psychology, and above all child psychology; the more so since we cannot hope that everybody would be in the happy situation of the teacher who reports in the " Pedagogical Seminary," the leading magazine for child study, that she brought a baby of three weeks into the class-room to demonstrate its smiling and crying and other functions of similar alarming interest. If we keep at a safe distance from such compromis-ing caricatures we can, I believe, expect highly valuable results from psychology instruction in the school.

But the possibility of teaching psychology in schools is not at all confined to regular courses about the whole subject; special chapters of psychology find a most natural place in the different fields of the usual school work. It is impossible to teach physics without discussing acoustical and optical sensations; the drawing teacher may discuss the conditions of our space perception or optical illusions or the seeing of colors; the study of history or literature not seldom brings with it a psychological analysis of the higher mental states, and a school child's curiosity rushes again and again to questions which only a sober knowledge of psychology can answer satisfactorily. It seems, therefore, not too much to demand that at least every high-school teacher should have some familiarity with the elements of psychology. He may be asked to teach it as a whole or he may be obliged to interweave parts of it with his other work; in any case he ought to have the facts of that science at his disposal as a material which he can teach like arithmetic or geography.

This alone would be for me sufficient reason for welcoming every future teacher to the college courses of psychology, but this attitude would not have the slightest relation to the other question, whether the teacher ought to know psychology for the purpose of making use of it for his professional methods of teaching. But we do not stand as yet before this latter question, which is much more complicated. If we follow up the different relations between psychology and the child, the question next in natural order will leave educational theory still out of the play.

II

We have asked so far what the child can learn from psychology; we must ask now what psychology can learn from the child. The question divides itself at once into many ramifications. Even if we abstract, as we planned to do, from all practical applications, and consider only the interests which psychology as a theoretical science can have in the child, we must from the start acknowledge two different points of view which are too often confused. The child's mind can be firstly the real object of psychological study, and secondly a vehicle for the study of the human mind in general, a tool in the hand of the psychologist. It is the same doubleness which we find, for instance, with regard to the pathology of mental life. The pathological mind as such can certainly be an important object of study, but it is such an object in the first place for the psychiatrist, not for the psychologist. The physician, of course, makes psychology as a whole serve the need of these pathopsychological cases which he analyzes in the hope of improving them. The psychologist, on the other side, attends to such abnormalities only as deviations from the normal soul, — variations which seem interesting to him only because they throw some new suggestive side light on the normal processes. He studies the disturbed harmony in the hope that the caricature-like exaggeration of special features will bring out a fuller understanding of their normal relations.

In exactly the same way we can approach the child's mind as an object worthy of our interest in and for itself, prepared to make use of our whole general psychological knowledge for the exploration of this new field; or we can turn to the mental life of children, with the purpose of finding through this study new paths of entrance to the old field of general human psychology. If the soul of the child is the object, all studies of this kind group themselves with inquiries about other sides of the nature of children, with the anthropology and physiology and pathology of the child; a bundle of investigations for which the name "child study" is perfectly correct, while to some ears the name

" paidology " seems to sound better. If, on the other hand, the child's mind becomes an instrument for investigating the phenomena and the laws of the mental mechanism, then of course the observation and experimentation on children is merely one of the many methods of empirical psychology, coördinated to the pathological and hypnotical and physiological and other methods which supplement by ways of indirect observation the direct self-observation of our laboratory work.   It forms then a narrower group together with the psychical studies of animals and primitive races, all aiding in the understanding of the complicated mental life of the highly developed adult man, by showing the different stages of ontogenetic and phylogenetic development.   Its special function can then well be compared with the service of embryology to general human anatomy.   If child study is an end in itself, every fact in the child's mental experiences is of equal importance or at least of equal scientific dignity ; if it is only a method in the service of psychology, science will carefully select only those facts by which the labyrinth of the developed mind becomes simpler and clearer while everything else remains indifferent.   If child study is the object, we start from our knowledge of the man to interpret the child ; if child research is a method, we seek knowledge about the child as a starting-point for our interpretation of the man.

This is, however, not the only point of view from which to classify the manifold efforts which are possible in this realm; it is the most central division, but it shows cross-sections with many other principles of division. The classification may, for instance, refer to the different stages of development, especially according as the time before or in or after school life is in question. But still more important: according as the observation goes on under natural conditions or under the artificial conditions of experiment; according as the inquiries are of individual character or seek for statistical results on the basis of large numbers; above all, according as the work is done by professional, at least specially prepared, psychologists or by psychological amateurs, who may be most excellent creatures in every other respect. Of course an exhaustive classification ought not to stop here. We can divide further; for instance, as the psychologists in question are such as have their theories beforehand or such as do not, and as the dilettants who observe the children are people who know that they do not know psychology or people who don't know even that.

The possible combination of all these factors secures such a manifoldness of types of research in this field that the mere collection of the results on the basis of coördination would contradict all principles of scientific methodology. If I may

be allowed a word of criticism, I should not
hesitate to claim that child study ought to be a
method and not an end; that it ought to be done
individually and not statistically, by professionals
and not by dilettants, more by natural observation and less by experiments. These decisions
hang, of course, closely together. If I take
paidology as a science by itself, then perhaps
I should also share that enthusiasm and delight over heaps of statistical and experimental
results which mothers, teachers, and nurses have
brought and certainly will bring together. But
all my instincts about the inner relations and
connections of human knowledge resist to the
utmost this artificial separation of child psychology from general psychology. I may write a
special book on the mental life of the child just
as I can write a monograph on memory or on hypnotism, but it has a final right of existence only in
virtue of its necessary place in the whole system
of psychology. To be sure, the chief reason for
taking this attitude lies in a conviction which I
must bring forward in the following discussion
again and again, and which is indeed the central
motive for my position in all these debates. I
shall indicate the point most quickly if I say:
Psychology is a study of mental facts, but not
every study of mental facts is therefore psychology. That psychology is a science and therefore every science psychology, probably nobody

pretends, and yet the logic of the conclusion would not be worse than that which is so often offered to us when every gathering or interpretation or statistics of mental facts is claimed as psychology. Most of the material which the friends of child study heap together is, even when mental facts and not physical ones are in question, nevertheless not psychology at all; and that small remainder which really contributes to a psychology of the child's mind belongs so clearly to general psychology that nobody would dream of an artificial separation if it were not usually so hopelessly mixed with unpsychological odds and ends.

Certainly the good appetite of psychology has sometimes become voracity in our days, and she has begun to devour all mental sciences, history and social life, ethics and logic, and finally, alas! metaphysics; but that is not a development, it is a disease and a misfortune. And when the necessary conflict between such high-handed psychology and the deep-rooted demands of the true life begins, such uncritical science must burst asunder. Psychology would learn too late that an empirical science can be really free and powerful only if it recognize and respect its limits, about which philosophy alone decides. The limits of psychology are easily understood. Psychology considers the mental life as an object which must be analyzed and explained, analyzed into elements and explained by laws. The psychologist, therefore, silently accepts the presupposition that the mental life is such an object and that this object is a combination of elements controlled in their connection by causal laws. In the reality of our inner experience our mental life has not at all these characteristics: the ideas are objects, while the feelings and volitions are subjective activities, and these objects are experienced as wholes and units, not as composita, and these activities as controlled by freedom, not by laws. Psychology thus presupposes for its purposes a most complicated transformation of the reality, and any attitude toward the mental life which does not need or choose this special transformation may be something else, but it is not psychology. Practical life and history, mental science and poetry, logic and ethics, religion and philosophy, all deal with mental life, but never with psychology as such. Not the material but the special standpoint characterizes the psychologist.

III

As soon as we are clear in regard to this elementary philosophical principle we cannot indeed doubt any longer that most of the so-called child psychology is partly history, partly economics and ethics, partly physiology, partly nothing at all, but is decidedly not psychology. To be fair I choose as illustration one of the very best investigations in the field, one which seems to me seriously interesting and important: the extended statistical studies about the stock of ideas which a child has when it enters the school. The differences between city and country children, between different home influences, between different nations, and so forth, come clearly to view, and the results suggest a continuation of these studies — but these results do not belong to psychology. The material of this inquiry is ideas, but these ideas not with regard to their constitution and their elements, but with regard to their practical distribution : it is not scientific botany to find out in whose yard in the town cherries, in whose yard apples grow. Suppose the same investigation made for adult persons : among a thousand men of fifty years of age how many have had impressions from such and such objects ? How many have seen a phonograph and how many a walrus ? The results would be a quite interesting contribution to the history of civilization, but nobody would think of classifying it under the psychology of the adult man, as we do not learn anything about the psychological structure and origin of an idea if we know that A happened to experience it while B never had a chance. Such an imitation of the so-called psychological studies on children by similar studies on adults will perhaps give us the

readiest insight into their real character. The
" Pedagogical Seminary " offers us a splendid
collection of the teasing and bullying phrases
which are in the mind of children, or it reports
with careful statistics that among 845 children
exactly 191 preferred wax dolls, 163 paper dolls,
153 china dolls, 144 rag dolls, 116 bisque dolls,
69 rubber dolls, and so on, or it studies the love
poems of boys and discovers that among 356
poems only 91 refer to the eyes, 50 to their expression, 41 to their color — blue leading with
22. We could choose just as well a hundred
other illustrations. Now let us try to repeat
such inquiries with adult men : let us find out
what preferences they have in cigarette-holders
and meerschaum pipes, or how often they refer
to the eyes in flirting, or what their disponible
material of nicknames and abusive words may
be. The results will not be much less instructive than those from the study of children, but
surely you would not call them psychology.

If we thus exclude everything which is not
really psychological, there still remains a good
set of problems which belong strictly to the
psychology of the child ; the analytic study
of its perceptions and associations, its memory
and attention, its feelings and emotions, its instincts and volitions, its apperceptions and judgments, to be described and explained with regard
to their elements and laws; but this group can

certainly not be separated from the psychology of the adult. There are the same elements and the same laws building up the mental life in all its different stages of development. The study of the child's mind then shows itself clearly as that which we claimed it to be: one of the many legitimate methods of studying the mental laws and elements in general. We could better have a special botany of the blossoms or a zoölogy of the eggs as scientific ends in themselves than a separated psychology of the children. On the other hand, if it is truly a method and vehicle of general mind study, then certain consequences are unavoidable. In the service of general psychology child study must first select its problems. What is the use of analyzing with the doubtful means of indirect observation those psychical states which we can find as the objects of direct observation in our own minds? Only that must be selected which allows us to push the analysis forward by showing our complicated states as preceded by simpler and simpler ones. But if the leading principle is thus a selection of material best fitted for clearing up the development of the complex combination of elements, it follows that the study of individual children is by far superior to the statistics in which the individual disappears, and that protracted observation is by far more important than the experimental investigation of a special

stage.   It follows, secondly, that the work must
be done by trained specialists or not at all.   That
child study which has for its aim only the collection of curiosities about the child, as an end in
itself, may be grateful to the nurse who writes
down some of the baby's naughty answers or to
the teacher who sacrifices half an hour of her
lesson to make experiments in the classroom to
fill out the blanks that are mailed to her.   The
students of that scientific child psychology which
stands in the service of the general mind study
know how every step in the progress of our science has depended upon the most laborious,
patient work of our laboratories and the most
subtle and refined methods, and that all this
seductive but rude and untrained and untech-
nical gathering of cheap and vulgar material
means a caricature and not an improvement of
psychology.   And it is not only the lack of technical training which brings these contributions
so near to hunting stories and their value for
scientific biology.   No, it is, above all, the absence of the psychological attitude.   That is in
my eyes not an opprobrium against the teacher.
I consider it to the teacher's credit that the
child is not an object of analysis for him, but I
blame those who make the teacher believe that
his observations nevertheless have value for psychology.
    Of course I know that some of the more sober

leaders of this movement emphasize very little the scientific value of such private adventurous expeditions of parents and school-teachers, and praise most highly the expected result that the teachers themselves get thus a more vivid interest in the children. I have to discuss this point later, and acknowledge here only that the young scholars themselves begin to doubt whether the gossip contained in these blanks means science or rubbish. Those who doubt, however, ought not to find comfort in the frequent comparison that the guileless teacher may collect the facts of the young souls like the wanderer who brings plants and stones home which the naturalist will use later as material. No, psychological material cannot be put into the pocket like a stone; it is not the fixation and communication of the found and perceived material only that have their difficulties, but the finding and perceiving themselves are in the highest degree dependent upon associations and theories already stored up.

Finally, even if all the stuff is reliable and truly psychological, still we ought not to exaggerate our hopes for real information. As long as the thousand little facts are not connected by a theory, the facts are dead masses, and if they are only illustrations of a theory, they do not teach us anything new. It will be a very exceptional case that a new insight into a law can be reached in this chance way;

physics, in spite of Bacon's recommendation, has certainly never reached anything in this way. At best the result will be a psychological commonplace. The "Pedagogical Seminary" prints 375 thoughts and reasonings observed in children, and true to its scientific intention it adds that this material is not sufficient. But I confess that I do not see what profit could possibly result for the psychologist from even three millions of such sayings. If we do not know the general facts of association, attention, apperception, and conception, then the whole material is mere gossip without psychological interest; and if we do know them and presuppose as a matter of course that the child has smaller experiences, fewer associations, and so on, then the material teaches us no more for the psychology of thought and reasoning than a collection of any 375 sentences of adult persons would do. Yet these nobody would think of reprinting. We ought not to deceive ourselves with trivialities. It is not science to make exact statistics of even the pebbles on the road or to collect the description of a hundred cases where the law of gravity was confirmed by the falling down of apples. Let us delay such luxury till the real duties of child psychology have been fulfilled; that is, till in the service of psychology the development of single mental functions, especially of self-consciousness, of the will, of the emotions, and of the ideas of space and time in individual children have been studied by really competent men with strictly scientific methods, a line of work in which our gratitude is due to Preyer, Perez, Stanley Hall, Baldwin, Sully, and other psychologists for a most valuable beginning.

The only part of the work for which I should welcome the coöperation of untrained observers is the search for, not the real study of, abnormal cases.   Pathological abnormalities in the child's mental life, in its emotions and imitations, its feelings and its will, are psychologically decidedly instructive, and the psychologist has no possibility of finding them if the layman does not draw his attention to them.   Such unusual deviations in full development strike the eye of every man ; no special psychological attitude is necessary.

Hitherto our question has been only to what extent theoretical psychology has an interest in children.   In practice, however, this simple issue becomes far more complicated by the hopes and fears which may be connected with this scientific work in the interest of the children and of their educators.   Of course psychology as such is not concerned in this question ; psychology does not work for a social premium and cannot be determined in its course by social anxieties.   But the psychologist, as a member of the social organism, has to adapt his endeavors to the needs of society; he must feel encouraged if he shares these social hopes and can feel himself an educational benefactor, and he will modify his officious disposition if he becomes convinced of the educational fears. The pessimistic group sees in all psychological experiments on children an unsound interference with their natural development, a kind of mental vivisection which, by its artificial stimulations and tensions, may become harmful to the health of the nervous system itself. Even observation under natural conditions seems to them of unfavorable influence on the *naïveté* and naturalness and modesty of the young subjects. Above all, they fear that the forced change of attitude in the teacher will do harm to the whole school life. In the interest of the teacher himself they add that such studies in the schoolroom burden the already overburdened man with work for which he himself does not feel sufficiently prepared; that he himself feels hampered by this new way of looking on the children, not as friends, but as interesting results of psychological laws; that he needs every minute of his school hours for his lessons, and that too often he confronts the dilemma, either to follow his educational conscience or to follow a superintendent who believes in the newest educational fad. The optimistic group of course holds to the exactly opposite view, sees no harm for the children, but the bliss of a deepened interest of the teachers in the children, and a subsequent lifting of the whole standard of school life. It is clear that such a background of antagonistic social movements complicates highly the theoretical problem. On the other hand, these hopes and fears about the practical effects of child psychology cannot be separated from the wider question what the teacher has to expect from psychology in general.

IV

Our plan to map out the whole manifoldness of antagonistic tendencies in the entire psycho-educational field brings us thus necessarily to a large group of new problems. We have discussed so far whether the child can study psychology directly, and secondly, whether psychology can directly study the child. We must now ask also whether psychology cannot have indirectly an influence on the child through the medium of the teacher; that is, whether the work of the teacher can be modified by psychology. But the question shows at once many important subdivisions; if we do not consider them, the result must be the confusion of Babel. The fact that we spoke before of the value of child psychology for the teacher, and are now discussing psychology in general, suggests from the start that we have to discriminate the different departments of our science. It may be that child psychology is educationally useless but physiological psychology excellent, or that experimental psychology is the elixir but rational psychology the poison of education. In any case, however, we have no right to throw all such methodologically separated parts of mind-study together and to decide about right or wrong in a wholesale manner. But another division of our question reaches still deeper: is psychology valuable to the teacher for his teaching methods directly, or only indirectly through the medium of a scientific educational theory? In the first case the teacher himself transforms his psychological knowledge into educational activity; in the other case educational theory has accomplished for him the crystallization of educational principles out of psychological substances, and he can follow its advice, perhaps, even without himself knowing anything about psychology. The two cases are so absolutely different that here, still more, an assenting or dissenting attitude toward the one proposition cannot have any significance at all with regard to the other. It may be just those who are convinced that the teacher ought to study education, and that education ought to make the fullest use of psychology, who form the strongest opponents of the psychologizing teacher who manufactures his private educational theory from his summer-school courses in experimental psychology. I shall therefore separate the two questions fully, and ask first, how far the individual teacher can make direct use of psychology for his teaching; and secondly, how far psychology is useful for the science of education.

I turn to the first question, which must now, as we have seen, be subdivided with regard to the different departments of possible mind study. A full exposition of the different parts of psychology and their complicated mutual relations would lead us, of course, far beyond the limits of this essay, but we cannot avoid giving our attention at least to some of the essential points. Of all the conceptions in question only that of child psychology does not need any further interpretation. We have seen that it does not by any means include every scientific interest with regard to the mental life of the child, but only those studies which consider its mental life under the categories of psychology, — that is, with regard to their elements and their causal laws; we have seen further that a child psychology of this type does not claim to be an end in itself, but only a method of general psychology.

Still simpler, if rightly understood, is the situation of "experimental psychology." Here there is still less doubt that it is separated from the other branches, not by its special objects, but

only by its special method — the experiment.
The frequent misunderstandings which exist arise
only when it is identified with indirect observation in opposition to self-observation, or is claimed
as a mathematical science in opposition to a
merely qualitative analysis, or is understood as
physiological psychology. All that is impossible.
In the first place, experimental psychology is so
little in opposition to self-observation that self-
observation forms really the largest part of experimental psychology; we can say that the whole
work of our modern psychophysical laboratories
must be characterized as essentially introspection,
but introspection under artificial conditions. To
be sure, experiments with indirect observation
also are possible, such as experiments on hypnotized subjects, on animals, and so forth, but they
are only exceptional guests in our laboratories.
Experimental psychology in any case exists wherever psychological observations, direct or indirect,
are made under artificial conditions chosen for
the special purpose of the observation. Secondly,
experimental psychology is so little a mathematical science that every hope of introducing mathematics, even into the smallest corner of it, must
readily be recognized as a failure in principle.
Psychical facts are not and cannot be measurable, and the more and less in our mental life
never means an addition of psychical elements;
we measure the physical conditions, but never

the mental facts themselves. Finally, experimental psychology is so far from identical with physiological psychology that we may even say that for its existence it does not need any relation to physiology at all. In our laboratories we study experimentally association and memory, attention and apperception, space sense and time sense, feelings and will, without being obliged to recognize officially that there exists a brain at all.

That brings us to the question of what physiological psychology is, as the latter statement presupposes a definition of the term with which not every one would agree. The word has indeed been used with quite different meanings. We can separate especially two types of use, a wider and a narrower one. In the wider sense of the word physiological psychology means the study of mental phenomena in their whole relation to physiological processes, central or peripheral, in the brain or in the sense organs, in the nerves or blood vessels or muscles. In the narrower sense it means only the study of the relation between the mental facts and the accompanying physiological brain processes. The merely terminological question is not essential for us, and it is indeed in part only terminological, as there cannot be any doubt that studies of both kinds are legitimate. Nevertheless there are good reasons for getting rid of the first use of the word and for sticking to the second. The first use

suggests clearly the mistaken idea that there
can be a psychology which does not refer, not
only for explanation but also for description and
analysis, at every moment to peripheral physical
facts.　This is not a defect or a caprice of our
present psychology ; for epistemological reasons
there can never be any analytic description of
psychical facts which does not refer directly or
indirectly to the physical objects which are in
relation to our organism.　The psychical fact as
such is just as indescribable as it is unmeasurable,
since it is the object which by its very nature
exists for one only and which remains therefore
ever incommunicable.　Every attempt to have a
science which describes mental facts must thus
at every stage relate the psychical facts to the
physical facts ; in short, there cannot be any empirical psychology at all which from beginning
to end is not simply physiological psychology in
the wider sense of the word.　The addition of
the word " physiological " has then no longer any
meaning ; it does not, if we think consistently,
mark any special group of studies, as it belongs
to all, and this whole is certainly better characterized by the epithet " empirical," which stands
over against " speculative," than by " physiological," which has no correlative and which we need
much more for a special group of psychophysiological problems.　The study of the mental
facts in their relation to the physiological brain

processes is indeed a scientific field by itself, with its own anatomical and physiological and pathological methods and with its own theoretical unity. But this field has an aspect quite different from what most people, and even most teachers, believe. They believe often that the analysis of psychical facts was in a poor and rather unscientific condition till the developed brain physiology, with its cells and fibres and gyri and centres, came and helped her poor relation. Really it is not at all so. Psychology knows endlessly more about these details than physiology, and in the development of the special psycho-physiological theories psychology has always led, and taught physiology how to interpret the chaos of brain facts. Brain physiology without psychology would have been perfectly blind, while psychology without detailed brain physiology would have stood exactly where it stands to-day, if we allow to psychology the general *a priori* postulate that every mental fact is the accompaniment of a physical process. This postulate is merely epistemological, and therefore independent of our knowledge of physiology. We must demand it because mental facts, as they are not quantitative, cannot enter into any causal equation. The demand for a causal interpretation of the mental life includes, therefore, the postulate that it must be transformed so that every element can be conceived as linked with a physiological process, but whether that process is going on in the occipital or in the parietal part of the brain is, for psychology, absolutely indifferent. In short, the whole physiological psychology consists of two factors : first, a general theory of psychophysiological relations which is based merely on philosophical and general biological principles and does not need physiology at all, and second, psychophysiological details which are important for the physiologist, but for psychology are a useless luxury. The special physiology of the brain, which in any case is still an almost unknown field, does not therefore help the psychologist anywhere; in my lectures on psychology before my students I hardly speak at all about the brain centres and the ganglion cells, and to base on them psychological insight turns our whole knowledge topsy-turvy.

V

The three usually vague and misinterpreted conceptions of child psychology, experimental psychology, and physiological psychology have now taken for us clear and sharp forms, and we understand the relative importance of their aims. We must now ask of what use they are for the individual teacher. My answer is simple and is the same for all the three branches : I maintain that they are not of the slightest use. Whether the special mental facts are in the one or the other gyrus of the brain, whether the development of the child's mind favors the one or the other theory about the constitution of a special mental phenomenon with regard to its psychophysical elements, and finally, whether laboratory experiments follow this or that track, are questions of absolutely no consequence to the teacher. Of course I have not the right to speak about my personal attitude, as I started to show objectively the opposing positions, but I confess in this case I do not see two sides at all. I do not see how any one can hope that the teacher will profit for his teaching methods from these three fields the moment they are correctly defined and are not mixed in the usual *mélange* with other things. Where a serious plea for them is made, always either the psychological fields are misinterpreted or the teacher is substituted for the science of education.

The case of physiological psychology is the simplest one. There was never a teacher who would have taught otherwise, or would have changed his educational efforts, if the physiological substratum of the mental life had been the liver or the kidneys instead of the brain. We have seen that here psychology has nothing at all to learn from physiology, and that it is a caricature of the facts if you tell the teacher that he can learn anything new about the mental life if he knows by heart the accompanying

brain processes ; and if the teacher, in the hope
of understanding the inner life of children better,
studies the ganglion cells under the microscope,
he could substitute just as well the reading of
Egyptian hieroglyphs. All talk about the brain
is, from the standpoint of the teacher, merely
cant, and I say this frankly at the risk of giving pleasure to those who do not deserve it — to
those who are only too lazy to study anatomy.

I insist that the situation lies in no way more
favorably for child psychology and experimental
psychology. Both sciences, as we saw, have as
their aim to be methods of analysis and explanation of the normal psychical facts. Child psychology reaches that goal by following up the
development; experimental psychology reaches it
by introducing artificial variations of the outer
conditions. Both have thus merely the one purpose, to aid our looking on mental life as if it
were a combination of elements, a composition
of psychophysical atoms. I know that such a
transformation of the inner life is extremely important for many scientific purposes, but I am
convinced, too, that such an atomizing attitude is
directly antagonistic to the attitude of the true
practical life, and thus opposed to the natural
instincts of the teacher toward his pupils. In
practical life our friends come in question for us
only as units ; their mental life interests us only
in so far as it means something to us and ex-

presses the real, willing personality.   Decompose
it for logical ends into its constructed elements of
atomistic sensations, and their sum is no longer
the inner life of our friend.   The naturalistic decomposition into elements is most valuable for its
purposes, but the purposes of life and friendship
and love and education are others.   There is no
necessary competition between these different
purposes ; that which serves the one is as true as
that which serves the other, because truth never
means a mere repetition of the one reality, but a
transformation of reality in the direction of logical ends.   The view of man as a free being, as
history must see him, is equally true with the
view of man as an unfree being, as psychology
must see him ; and the friends' and educators'
view of the child as the indissoluble unit and
willful personality is just as valuable and true as
the psychologist's view which sees it as a psychophysical complex mechanism.   You destroy
a consistent psychology if you force on it the
categories of practical life, but you also destroy
the values of our practical life if you force on
them the categories of psychology.   In experimental psychology, or in child psychology, the
emotion may show itself as composed of circulatory and muscular elements, and the will as made
up from muscle and joint and skin sensations ;
but if you offer such transformed product to the
teacher, you do worse than if you should offer to

a thirsty man one balloon filled with hydrogen
and another with oxygen instead of a good swal-
low of water.   The chemist is quite right : that
is water ; the fainting man insists that it is not,
and life speaks always the language of the thirsty.

Do I mean by all this that the teacher ought
to be without interest in the mental life of the
children, a dull and indifferent creature without
sympathy for the individualities and desires and
characteristics of the pupils?   Just the contrary
is true.   I detest this mingling of the teacher
with psychology just because I do not wish to
destroy in him the powers of sound and natural
interest.   It has been my point from the start
that not every interest in mental life is psychology, but that psychology studies mental life from
a special point of view.   I therefore separated
child psychology sharply from other kinds of
interest in children's minds, and the psychological sciences from the historical and normative
sciences.   Certainly the teacher ought to study
children and men in general, but with the
strictly anti-psychological view ; he ought to acknowledge them as indissoluble unities, as centres of free will the functions of which are not
causally but teleologically connected by interests
and ideals, not by psychophysical laws.   The
study of the mental life of man from this other
point of view is not a special science ; it belongs
partly to history and literature, partly to logic

and ethics and philosophy, partly to poetry and religion. Here may the teacher wander at his ease, and he will learn to understand man, while psychology teaches him only to decompose man. Have you never observed what bad judges of men in real life the psychologists are, and what excellent judges of men the history-makers and historians are? Not a little of this desirable knowledge about the real inner man and his unity of intentions may be found also in the so-called "rational psychology." To be sure, in its deductions it is often too dependent upon metaphysics, and, above all, we must not forget that, strictly speaking, it is not psychology at all, since it aims at synthesis, not at analysis ; but it is full of that which the teacher needs : suggestions to intensify interest for the child's mind by a deeper understanding of its volitional relations, and by a critical appreciation of mental values for the inner life. The teacher needs interest in the mental life from the point of view of interpretation and appreciation; the psychologist, with his child psychology and experimental and physiological psychology, gives him and must give him only description and explanation. Pestalozzi and Froebel were no psychologists.

This standpoint does not at all exclude the existence of facts which demand that the teacher change his attitude and consider the child from

the naturalistic atomistic psychophysical point of
view; and for this case also the teacher ought to
be prepared. I have in mind the facts related
to physical and mental health. To be sure, the
questions of hygiene, of light and air and re-
freshment and fatigue, of normal sense organs
and muscles, as well as of normal mental functions, of pathological instincts and emotions, abnormal inhibitions and mental diseases, are by
a hundred threads connected with the schoolroom, and there is not the slightest doubt that
they have to be treated from the psychophysical
point of view. That is no inconsistency; these
facts belong indeed to an absolutely different
system of relations, which has to be cared for,
but which is not the system of educational relations. The word which I am writing now belongs to the stream of my thoughts and at the
same time to the stream of my fountain pen — I
have to take care of both. In the moment
when the teacher takes care of the child's myo-
pia or hysteria he is not teacher but psychophysiological adviser of the child, just as it is not
my function as a scholar to fill my fountain pen.
Nobody overlooks that it is extremely important
for society that the teacher should be well prepared to fulfill this naturalistic function, too.
Much misfortune could be avoided if every
teacher were especially trained to recognize
pathological disturbances of the mind in their

first beginnings, and for that he would indeed need some real psychology. Only do not say that he needs the psychology as teacher, while he may remain a good teacher in spite of the psychology which he studies in the service of hygiene.

VI

This last discussion referred only to the question how far psychology interests the individual teacher as a help in his efforts, but that was only one side of the more general problem, how far psychology can be helpful to education. There remains the other side : how can psychology influence education through the mediating channel of a scientific educational theory; and it is clear that here again the questions are so independent of each other that a mixture of the two must result in confusion. We can be convinced that the view of the teacher ought not to be psychological, and we can nevertheless demand that education as science make the fullest possible use of every branch of psychology. Exactly that has always been, and is to-day, my hope.

To be sure, the impression which theories of education make in our day is in no way overwhelming. The demand for educational wisdom is decidedly greater than the supply, and neither great systems nor imposing thoughts characterize the pedagogy of our age. The whole educational trade does its business to-day with small coin. Our time needs a man like Herbart again. But at least one very favorable condition for the strong development of education is given : the widespread conviction that we need it. No previous time has so seriously called for a specialistic help from scientific education, and if, for want of revolutionizing great thoughts, we demand anything from it, then we demand that it shall carefully make use of the whole empirical knowledge of our time to transform it into suggestions for the teacher. A responsible administration will then further transform these suggestions into obligatory prescriptions. Among this empirical knowledge which education unites into a new practical synthesis psychology certainly plays one of the most important rôles in determining the means by which the educational ends can be worked out. There is no reason to confine this to a special branch of psychology; all that the analytical study of mind offers by experimental or physiological methods, by self-observation or by statistics, by child psychology or by pathology, by " old " or by " new " means, in short, the best and fullest psychology of the time has to be one of the tools in the workshop of education. The educational scholar differs in two essential respects clearly from the individual teacher. First, while the teacher's practical attitude must suffer, as we saw, by the influence of the antagonistic psychological attitude in the same consciousness, the theoretical scholar, who is not himself a teacher, can of course easily combine the two attitudes and alternate between them. The teacher must live fully in the one attitude, and every opposite impulse inhibits him; the student of education remains in a theoretical relation to each of them, and can therefore easily link them. He can take the whole wisdom of psychology and physiology and remold it into suggestions for the practical teaching attitude. The teacher ought thus to receive finally, indeed, the influence of psychology, but only if the causal facts are transformed by some one else beforehand into teleological connections, adapted to the teacher's unpsychological work. The bread which the teacher bakes for his classes comes indeed partly from the wheat on psychological fields, but the corn must be ground beforehand in the educational mills. And the second point is not less important: such transformation of psychological investigations into ideas how to teach may successfully be done by the steady coöperation of a large number of specialists who make a whole lifework of it, but absolutely never by a single teacher. He may run through laboratories and digest statistical tables; he may commit to memory the numberless papers of the periodicals and feast on microscopical ganglion cells, but nowhere will he find anything which suggests really a whole plan or a straight impulse. A thousand little odds and ends without the slightest unity will be in his hand, and if he really believes himself to have the material for a little prescription, then he probably does not see how directly it contradicts other indications. It is impossible for him to survey the whole field, and nobody can ask him to do privately, by the way, a work which would give sufficient occupation to a whole generation. Even the slightest progress in the field presupposes a full acquaintance with the whole literature of the special subject. We cannot demand that from the much-burdened practical teacher, even for any one problem; how absurd to hope it for all those which he practically needs: for memory and attention, for imagination and intellect, for emotion and will, for fatigue and play, and a hundred other important functions. Do we not lay a special linking science everywhere else between the theory and practical work? We have engineering between physics and the practical workingmen in the mills; we have a scientific medicine between the natural sciences and the physician. If a man prepared with the most wonderful knowledge of the anatomy, physiology, pathology, and chemistry of the century should begin medical practice and write prescriptions without having passed through a training in real medicine, he would be either the wildest quack, curing one organ at the expense of a dozen others, or he would throw away his theoretical wisdom and follow his practical instincts. The ten thousand little laboratory experiments he knows would only confuse him if a whole generation of medical men had not, in specialistic coöperation, worked them up for practical use. Only, two points such a theory of education must not overlook.

On the one hand, education forgets too easily that such psychophysical material is only a part of the stuff to be mixed and filtered and brought into solution before educational principles are crystallized. The causal analysis of the psychophysical variations and possibilities must at every point be combined with the teleological interpretation of the ends suggested by ethics and æsthetics, by history and religion. It is not enough to substitute for a serious study and examination of the latter half a mere personal taste and capricious instinct, which takes as a matter of course that which ought to be scientifically criticised. Carelessness in the teleological part makes the synthesis just as dilettantic and useless as ignorance about the causal material. Nothing ought there to be taken for granted. Take one simple illustration instead of a thousand. The statistics show a very poor knowledge of the natural objects of the country on the part of the youngest school children. The investigator draws the educational conclusion that preparation in that respect must be improved. But who gives us a scientific right to take for granted that early acquaintance with natural objects is at all desirable? Socrates did not think so; not the stones but only men can teach us. The best education is certainly not that which gives a little bit of everything. We must develop some and must inhibit other psychological possibilities; psychology as such cannot decide on that. Only when education succeeds really in amalgamizing the two sides, and becomes something else than merely picked-out psychology, can we tell the teacher that he will find that study of man which he desires not only in philosophy and history and literature, but also in the handbooks and seminaries of education.

But education must appreciate a second point also. It cannot expect to find all necessary psychological and physiological information always ready-made. As no science is merely a collection of scraps, psychology as such cannot examine every possible psychological fact in the universe, but must select just those which are essential for the understanding of the psychical elements and laws. This choice in the interest of psychology differs of course fully from the choice of psychical facts which education would make for its own purposes. Here the science of education must take the matter in its own hand and must work up, with all the subtle means and methods of modern psychology, those psychological phenomena which are important for the special problems; the most intimate relation to psychological laboratories is here a matter of course. In what form education will fulfill this demand may itself be at first a matter of educational experiment. Some believe in special psycho-educational experimental laboratories, some believe in special experimental schools, and recently the proposition was made for the appointment of special school psychologists attached to the superintendent's office in large cities. In any case the work has to be done; the psychologist as such cannot do it, and the teacher cannot do it, either. For the psychologist it would be a burden, for the teacher it would be a most serious danger; the student of education alone can do it. Of course even these adjuncts of superintendents, and these principals of experimental schools, must never forget that their work always refers only to the one half, which is misleading without the other half — to the causal system, which must be harmonized with the teleological one.

Personally I consider the psycho-educational laboratory as the most natural step forward.

Such laboratories would be psychophysical laboratories, in which the problems are selected and adjusted from the standpoint of educational interest. All that has been done so far in our psychological laboratories for the study of attention, memory, apperception, imagination, and so on, in spite of seductive titles, has almost never had anything to do with that part of these functions which is essential for the mental activities of the classroom. While the individual teacher, as we have seen, ought to keep away from our psychological laboratories because our attitude is opposed to his, the student of education ought to keep away from us because, in spite of the same attitude, we have too seldom problems belonging to his field. It is a waste of energy to hunt up our chronoscope tables and kymograph records for little bits of educational information which the psychologist has brought forward by chance; sciences cannot live from the chances of work which is intended for other purposes. When in the quiet experimental working place of the psycho-educational scholar, through the steady coöperation of specialists, a real system of acknowledged facts is secured, then the practical attempts of the consulting school psychologist and of the leader of experimental classrooms have a safer basis, and their work in its turn will help the theoretical scholar till the coöperation of all these agents produces a practical education which the teacher will accept without experimenting himself. Then the teacher may learn psychology, to understand afterward theoretically the educational theory he is trained in, but he himself has not to make educational theory nor to struggle with psychological experiments.

There need be no fear that such psycho-educational laboratories would have too few problems at their disposal; a fear which may be suggested by the fact that the friends of this movement always refer to the same few show pieces, the experiments on fatigue, on memory, and on association. The situation would develop just as twenty-five years ago did that of experimental psychology, which itself lived at first only from the crumbs that fell from the table of other sciences — physics and physiology. It also began with only a few chance questions, with the threshold of sensations and reaction times; but since it has wrought in its own workshops, for its own points of view and interests, it has conquered the whole realm of psychology. In the same way psycho-educational experiments will extend the work to all the functions active in education. Such new studies will then show how incomplete an essay like this is, and how many other relations still exist between the child and the study of mental life. But even this incomplete enumeration is sufficient to show at

least one thing: the question whether there is
a connection between psychology and education
cannot be answered simply with yes or no, but
must be answered by firstly, secondly, thirdly,
fourthly — I do not discuss whether we can ever
say also: lastly.

PSYCHOLOGY AND ART

I

COMMON sense, which is to-day, as it has been since eternity, merely the trivialized edition of the scientific results of the day before yesterday, is just now on the psychological track. The scientists felt some years ago that the psychological aspect of the products of civilization was too much neglected, and that the theoretical problem how to bring the creations of social life under the categories of psychology might find some new and interesting answers in these days of biological, physiological, experimental, and pathological psychology. Thus the scientific study of the psychology of society and its functions has made admirable progress. Science, of course, took this only as a special phase of the matter; it did not claim to express the reality of language and history, law and religion, economics and technics, in describing and explaining them as psychological facts. Therefore science did not forget the more essential truth that civilization belongs to a world of purposes and duties and ideals; at present, indeed, science

emphasizes decidedly this latter view, and has
changed the direction of its advance.   Common
sense, as usual, has not yet perceived this
change of course.   Ten years may pass before
it finds it out.   Above all, one-sided as ever,
common sense has misunderstood the word of
command, as if the psychological aspect must
be taken as the only possible aspect, and as if
psychology could reach the reality.   Therefore
common sense marches on, still waving the flag
of psychology, and with it its regular drum
corps, the philistines.

This pseudo-philosophical movement, which
takes the standpoint of the psychologist wrongly
as a philosophical view-point of the whole inner
world, has found perhaps nowhere else so little
organized resistance as in the realm of art; for
the real artist does not care much about the
right or wrong theory.   For the same reason,
indeed, it may seem that just here the influence
of a warped theory must be very indifferent
and harmless.   A one-sided theory of crime may
mislead the judge, who necessarily works with
abstract theoretical conceptions ; but a one-sided
psychological theory of art cannot do such harm,
as the artist relies in any case on the wings of
his imagination, and mistrusts the crutches of
theories.   This would certainly be the case if
there did not exist three other channels through
which the wise and the unwise wisdom can influ-

ence, strengthen, and inhibit the creative power
of art.

The market influence is one way; that is a
sad story, but it is not the most important factor, as the tragedy of the market depends much
more upon practical vulgarity than upon theoretical mistakes. Æsthetical criticism is another
way; but even that is not the most dangerous,
as it speaks to men who ought to be able to
judge for themselves, although nobody doubts
that they do not do so. The most important of
the three, however, is art education in the
schoolroom. Millions of children receive there
the influence that is strongest in determining
their æsthetical attitude; millions of children
have there the most immediate contact with the
world of the visible arts, and mould there the
sense of refinement, of beauty, of harmony.
Surely the drawing-teacher can have an incomparable influence on the æsthetic spirit of the
country, — far greater than critics and million-
aire purchasers, greater even than the professional art schools. The future battles against
this country's greatest enemy, vulgarity, will be
fought largely with the weapons which the drawing-teachers supply to the masses. Whoever has
attended their meetings or examined the exhibi-
tions of schoolroom work knows that they do
not lack enthusiasm and industry, and that their
importance in the educational system is growing

rapidly. But they are primary teachers, and primary teachers are men who adore nothing more than recently patented theories which appeal to common sense; to-day they really feast on psychology. The greater the influence, the more dangerous is every wrong step on the theoretical line, the more necessary a sober inquiry as to how far all this talk about psychology and art really covers the ground.

We thus raise the question, what psychology and art have to do with each other, in its most general form, at first without any relation to the practical problems. If we acknowledge the question in such an unlimited form, we cannot avoid asking, as a preamble to the discussion, whether the work of art cannot be itself a manual of psychology; whether, especially, the poet ought not to teach us psychology. We all have heard often that Shakespeare and Byron, Meredith and Kipling, are better psychologists than any scholar on the academic platform, or that Henry James has written even more volumes on psychology than his brother William. That is a misunderstanding. The poet, so far as he works with poetic tools, is never a psychologist; if modern novelists of a special type sometimes introduce psychological analysis, they make use of means which do not belong to pure art; it is a mixed style which characterizes decadence.

It is true that discussion would be meaning-

less if we were ready to call every utterance
which has to do with mental life psychology.
Psychology does not demand abstract scientific
forms; it may be offered in literary forms, yet
it means always a special kind of treatment of
mental life. It tries to describe and to explain
mental life as a combination of elements. The
dissolution of the unity of consciousness into
elementary processes characterizes psychology,
just as natural science demands the dissection
of physical objects; the appreciation of a physical object as a whole is never natural science,
and the interpretation and suggestion of a mental state as a whole is never psychology. The
poet, as well as the historian and the man of
practical life, has this interpretation of the whole
as his aim; the psychologist goes exactly the
opposite way. They ask about the meaning,
the psychologist about the constitution; and the
psychological elements concern the poet as little
as the microscopical cells of the tree interest the
landscape painter. The tree in the painting
ought, indeed, to be botanically correct; it
ought not to appear contradictory to the results
of the botanist's observations, but these results
themselves need not appear in the painting. In
the same way, we demand that the poet create
men who are psychologically correct, — at least
in those cases in which higher æsthetical laws
do not demand the psychological impossibilities

of fairyland, which are allowed like the botani-
cal impossibilities of conventionalized flowers or
the anatomical impossibilities of human figures
with wings. We detest the psychologically
absurd creations of the stage villain and the
stage hero in third-class melodrama, the psychological marionettes of newspaper novels, and
the frequent cases of insanity in poor fiction,
for which the schooled psychologist would make
at once the diagnosis that there must be simula-
tion in them, as the insane never act so. We
demand this psychological correctness, and the
great poet instinctively satisfies it so fully that
the psychologist may acknowledge the creations
of poetry as substitutional material for the psychical study of the living man. The psychologist believes the poet, and studies jealousy from
Othello, and love from Romeo, and neurasthenia
from Hamlet, and political emotions from Cæsar;
but the creation of such lifelike men is in itself
in no way psychology.

The poet creates mental life in suggesting it
to the soul of the reader; only the man who
decomposes it afterward is a psychologist. The
poet works as life works; the child who smiles
and weeps causes us to think of pleasure and
pain too, but it offers us no psychological understanding of pleasure and pain. Just so the poet
smiles and weeps, and if he is a great artist, with
strong suggestive power, he forces our minds to

feel with him, while we have only an intellectual interest if he merely analyzes the emotions and gives us a handful of elements determined by abstract psychological conceptions. Popular language calls a poet a good psychologist if he creates men who offer manifold material for the analysis of the psychologist; when the poet begins to make that analysis himself, and to explain with the categories of physiological psychology why the hero became a dreamer, and the dreamer a hero, and the saint a sinner, he will hinder his scientific effort by the desire to be a poet, and will weaken his poetry by his instructive side show. Meredith and Bourget do it, Ibsen never. Poetry and psychology are different, not because they speak a different language, but because they take an absolutely different attitude toward the mental life; the wisdom of the poet about the human soul does not belong to a handbook of psychology. For music and the visible arts the whole question is non-existent, or at least ought not to exist. A side branch of it, nevertheless, continues to grow in the old discussion whether music ought to "describe" the human feelings. The confusion about the logical meaning of description here lies more on the surface; theoretically the case is the same as in poetry. The composer describes the emotions as little as the poet does; tones and verses suggest the feelings, while it is an unmusical, unpoetical business to psychologize about them; but just that is our aim, if we consider the preamble as closed, and ask once more what art has to do with psychology.

II

We have seen so far that art is not by itself psychology; the remaining question, in which all centres, is, then, how far art can become an object of psychology. The situation is simple. Psychology is the science which describes and explains the mental processes. A physical thing or process, even a brain action, is never, therefore, an immediate object of psychology. Every work of art — the pencil drawing and the written poem, the played melody and the sculptured statue — exists as a physical thing; hence the work of art itself is never an object of psychology, and the description of it lies outside of the psychologist's province. The physicist describes the tone waves of a melody; the geometrician describes the lines and curves and angles of a drawing. The physical object is in contact with the human mind at two points: at its start and its goal. Every work of art springs from the mind of the artist, and reaches the mind of the public; its origin and its effect are both psychical processes, and both are material for the description and explanation of the psychologist. Two groups of psychological problems are thus offered, — two points of view for the psychological study of art; a third one cannot exist. The one asks, By what psychological processes does the mind create art? The other asks, By what psychological processes does the mind enjoy art?

Modern psychology has attained to its rapid progress of late years through the wonderful development of its methods; it believes no longer that one way alone will bring us to the goal; we have to adapt the methods to the problem. It is quite clear that these two æsthetical psychological problems demand different methods. The question how the artist creates art lies beyond the self-observation of the psychologist; he must go back to the past. The question how the work of art influences the enjoying spectator can be studied by an analysis of his own æsthetical emotions. In the interest of this self - observing analysis he may introduce experimental methods, but he cannot make experiments with the artistic production. On the other hand, the artistic creative functions may easily be traced down toward the art of the child, of the primitive races, even of the animals. And so the first group of investigations makes use chiefly of the sociological, biological, and historical methods of psychology; the second group favors experimental methods. The larger material is at the disposal of the first group; the

more exact treatment characterizes the second.
We cannot sketch the results here even in the
most superficial outlines; we can recall only the
most general directions which these studies have
taken.

First, the psychology of the art-creating process.   The æsthetical psychologist, in our days
of Darwinism, goes back to the play of animals.
Biologically this is easily understood; the frequent playful contests are a most valuable training for action, — as necessary, therefore, for the
organism in the struggle for existence as is any
other function of the nervous system, and yet
they contain the most important elements of
æsthetic creation : they are actions which are
useless for the present state of the organism,
carried out for enjoyment only.   Social psychology finds the more complicated forms of the
same impulses in the life of savages.   We see
how the primitive races accompany their work
by rhythmical songs, how their dances stir up
lyrical poetry, how their tools and vessels and
weapons and huts become decorated, how art
springs from the religious and social and technical life.   The psychologist links these first
traces of art with the productions of civilized
peoples.   His interest is not that of the philo-
logical historian ; he does not care for the single
work of art as the unique occurrence ; no, he
looks for the psychological laws which under the

varying circumstances produce just the given
works of poetry and sculpture, of music and
architecture and painting. We learn to understand how climate and political conditions, technical, material, and social institutions, models
and surrounding nature, brought it about that
Egypt and China and India, or Greece and Italy
and Germany, had just their own development
of artistic production. Art becomes thus an
element of the social consciousness, together
with law and religion, science and politics; but
art is psychologically still more interesting than
any other function of the national soul, because
it is less necessary for the biological existence
than any other production of man. Art is therefore freer, follows more easily every pressure
and tension, every inner tendency and outer
opportunity; it can fully disappear even in the
strongest social organism, and can break out in
fullest glory even in the weakest sociological
body. It is in its incomparable manifoldness
and easiness of adaptation that art shows best
how the mental products of man are dependent
upon the totality of variable conditions.

While such a sociological view contrasts different periods and nations, psychology does not
overlook the differences among individuals. The
general artistic level of the whole social mind
is only one side of the problem; the variation of individuals above and below this level,

from the anti-æsthetic philistine to the greatest
genius, is the other side, and here also the dependence upon the most diverse conditions at-
tracts interest.   The psychologist consults biography, especially the autobiographies of poets
and painters, and follows up most carefully the
subtle influences which fertilized the imagination and gave abnormal direction to the personality.

Studying thus the artistic production in individuals at all times and at all places, psychology
finally abstracts a general understanding of the
creative process and its conditions.   There appears nothing mysterious in it: by manifold
threads it seems connected with the mental functions of simple attention, with inhibition and
suggestion; in other directions with dreams and
illusions, and also with the abnormal functions
of hypnotism and insanity.   It is a most complex process, truly, in which the whole personality is engaged, but it is connected by short steps
with so much simpler events in mental life, and
it can so easily be traced back to the artistic elements in the child, that the psychologist has no
reason to despair; the artistic function of the
brain is not beyond the causal understanding.
The machinery of modern psychological conceptions, the atomistic sensations and their laws of
association and inhibition, can theoretically explain it in its entirety from the schoolboy's

drawing of profiles on his blotting-paper up to
Michael Angelo's decoration of the dome of St.
Peter's with immortal religious frescoes.

III

Very different indeed are the methods by
which we investigate our second group of æsthetical problems, the psychological effect of the
beautiful object.   Experimental psychology enters here into its rights.   When the students of
mental life, twenty years ago, took up the exact
method of natural science and worked out experimental schemes for the most refined analysis
of psychical processes, it seemed at first a matter
of course that only the intellectual processes,
especially the functions of perception, and perhaps the elementary activities, would offer themselves to such inquiries.   But slowly the new
method has reached and conquered one field
after another, — memory and imagination, association and apperception, feeling and emotion,
undeveloped and abnormal mental states; and
now, in different places, experimental work is
dealing with the most delicate psychical fact, the
æsthetical feeling and its conditions.

Fechner gave a strong impulse to such an experimental study of æsthetic elements a long
time ago.   He asked systematically a large number of persons which one of a set of rectangles,
for instance, each of them preferred; the ten

forms varied from a square to a rectangle with a length of five and a breadth of two inches. He found a marked æsthetical preference for those forms which are determined by the golden section; that is, in which the short side stands to the long side as the latter stands to the sum of both. To-day the work transcends in every direction such elementary beginnings. In the first place, it is not confined to a special art. Music and poetry share equally with the visible arts. The æsthetical harmony and discord of tones, their relation to beats and overtones, to the fusion and the discrimination of tones, to timbre and duration; in the same way, the musical properties of rhythm, its relations to the attention and time sense, to the physiological processes of breathing and muscle tension, and to many other psychophysical functions, — all these have become the problems of the experimental psychologist. These studies of musical rhythm naturally turn the attention toward the elements of poetry; the experimental study of rhythm in the verse, and its relation to the position of the rhyme, to the length of the stanza, to the fluctuations of apperception, to the physiological functions, and so forth, is exceedingly promising, although still in its beginning.

Much more developed is the attempt to reach experimentally the characteristics of the visible arts. Material and form, above all color and shape, offer themselves in an unlimited series of problems. The color spectrum has always been at home in the laboratory, but the psychologist has studied color as an element of perception or as a function of the eye, not as the object of æsthetical feeling. His studies now take a new direction and ask which of two colors is preferred. How does this preference depend upon saturation, brightness, extension? What combination of colors is agreeable : how does this effect depend upon the relative extension of the colored surface; how upon the colored materials and the relation between their intensity or their whiteness? Which shapes and angles and sections are preferred : how does this preference depend upon associations, or upon our bodily position, or upon eye movements? How does the plastic effect, in stereoscopic vision for example, influence the intensity of æsthetic feeling; how does movement influence it, or the combination of shape with color? In a series of rectangles or ellipses or bisected lines, is only one of them agreeable, or has the curve of our æsthetical pleasure several maximal points?

The experimental investigation may come much nearer still to the problem of fine arts. I take as illustration a series of experiments which make up part of a recent thesis from the Harvard laboratory. The problem is the pleasing balance of two sides of an æsthetic object. That is, of course, realized in the simplest way by geometrical symmetry as many works of architecture show it; we have this pleasing feeling of equilibrium, also, when we see a well-composed building of which the two halves are far from identical, and every painting shows this ideal symmetry of composition without the monotony of geometrical uniformity; so it is even in the most irregular Japanese arrangement. The question arises under what conditions this demand for balance is fulfilled, if the objects in both halves are different. Translated into the methods of experimental psychology, the question would be, how far, for instance, a long vertical line must be from the centre of a framed field, if a line of half its length is at a given distance from the centre on the other side; how far if a point or a curve of special form or two lines are there. The variations are endless. In an absolutely dark room is a framed field of black cloth, which is so illuminated that no other object in the room is visible; by a little device, bright lines, points, curves, also letters, pictures, objects, can be made to move over this field without showing the moving apparatus, while the exact position of each is indicated on a scale. One line may be given on the left side, and the experimenter has to find the most pleasing position of a double line on the other, imitating thus the case when two figures are to be on one side of a painting, while one only is to balance them on the other side; where must it stand? Starting from such simple lines, the investigation turns to more complicated questions: What is the influence of the impression of depth? — for instance, a flat picture on one side, a picture representing depth on the other. What is the influence of interest? — a meaningless paper on one side, a paper of equal size with interesting figures on the other side. What is the influence of apparent movement? — a picture of a resting object on one side, an equally large object which suggests movement in a special direction on the other. So the problem can easily be carried to a complication of conditions which does justice to the manifoldness of principles involved in the composition of paintings, sculptures, decorations, interiors, buildings, and landscapes. If, finally, all these experiments are carried out under different subjective conditions, in different states of bodily position, of eye movement, of distance, of attention, of fatigue, under different degrees of illumination, with different colors, with different associations, all with different subjects and in steady relation to the real objects of historical art, we learn slowly to understand our æsthetic pleasure in the balance of a composition, and its relation to the functions of our body.

Some one may say: All these experiments are too simple; they may be quite interesting, but they never reach the complication of real art. What are those simple figures beside a Madonna, those primitive harmonies beside a symphony? Yet is it a reproach to the physicist that he studies the nature of the gigantic thunderstorm, not from an equally large electrical discharge, but from the tiny sparks of his little laboratory machine? And if the physicist is interested in the waves of the ocean, he studies the movements in a small tank of water in his working-room, and introduces simple artificial movements. It is just the elementary character of experimental methods which guarantees their power for explanation; and æsthetical effects can be psychologically understood only if we study their elements in the most schematic way possible. The necessary presupposition is, of course, that the æsthetical attitude itself can be maintained in the laboratory rooms, and there is no reason for being skeptical about that. With regard to practical emotions such skepticism may be correct: we cannot love and hate, nor admire and detest in the laboratory, and it may even be said that the joy of the laboratory is not agreeable, and the pain is not painful. But the æsthetical emotion remains intact precisely on account of the absence of every practical relation in it. The beautiful or the ugly thing lasts as such in every corner of our workshop.

The experimental study of the psychological effect of art seems thus even more safely housed than the biological and historical study of the psychological production of art, and both together form already a psychological system of æsthetics which certainly still has blanks, but which is surprisingly near completeness. Psychology will go on in this way till the most delicate cause and the most subtle effect of each artistic work are understood by the action of causal laws, like any other cause and effect in nature.

IV

Before us lies the question which is important for the teacher: how far the results of such studies can become productive, or at least suggestive, for instruction in artistic drawing. Here again we must separate the two sides, — the causes and the effects of the beautiful objects. The causes which produce the drawing are the activities of the pupil; the effects are the impressions on the spectator. The study of the causes will help us to understand how to train the æsthetical activities of the pupil; the study of the effects will help us to advise how the drawing or painting should be made up in order to please others. The study of the causes suggests to us methods of teaching; the study of the effects suggests rules and facts which are

to be taught.   The study of the causes interests
only the teacher who handles the pupil; the
study of the effects offers insight which the
teacher may share with the pupil.

Think first of the effects.   Psychology has
analyzed the impressions on our sense of beauty,
and each fact must express a rule which can
be learned.   Blue and red are agreeable, blue
and green are disagreeable: therefore combine
red and blue, but not green and blue.   The
golden section of a line is the most agreeable of
all divisions: therefore try to divide all lines,
if possible, according to this rule.   Such psychological prescriptions hold, of course, for all
arts: do not make verses with lines of ten feet;
do not compose music in a scale of fifths.   Step
by step we come to the prescription for a tragedy, for a symphony, for a Renaissance palace;
how much more for the details of a simple drawing!   Fill the space thus and thus; take care of
good balance; if there is a long line on one
side, make the short line on the other side nearer
to the centre: these are æsthetical prescriptions
which can be learned and exercised like the laws
of perspective for architectural drawing.   Whenever the pupil follows the rules, his drawing will
avoid disagreeable shocks to the spectator.   I
am free, I trust, from the suspicion that I over-
estimate the value of experimental psychology
for teachers; I have often attacked its misuses.

Here the case is quite different. Such prescriptions do not prescribe the ways of teaching, but are material of instruction. There is no other school subject for which psychology supplies such material. Mathematics and natural sciences, languages and history, are not learned in school with reference to their psychological effects. Art, however, has an absolutely exceptional position. My belief, therefore, that methods of teaching cannot be learned to-day from the psychological laboratory is no contradiction of my acknowledgment that artistic prescriptions, worthy to be taught, can be deduced from psychology. I see with great pleasure that the development in this direction goes steadily on, and that children learn easily and joyfully the ways of avoiding ugly lines and arrangements.

My theoretical objections against teaching on the basis of psychological knowledge interfere much more with the pedagogical results which may perhaps be indicated by the study of the psychological causes of art. If we apply here our theoretical insight at all, the result cannot have the form, Teach your pupils to make the drawing thus and so; but the form, Teach thus and so your pupils to make a drawing. If we understand the causes which produce a beautiful drawing, and if by our teaching we can influence the central system of the child so that the causes for such production are established, then

it seems that the goal is reached. But we are
not only far from a full understanding; we are
endlessly farther from such desired influences.
To know the chemical constitution of an egg
does not mean the power to produce an egg
which can be hatched. We cannot make a
genius, we cannot make talent; and by itself the
psychological analysis only indicates, and that but
slightly, how to evolve from a bad draughtsman
a good one. We may make the general abstraction that constant training is a good thing; to
reach such a triviality, however, we need psychology as little as we need scientific physiology to
find out that eating is useful for our nourish-
ment. Wherever psychological speculation goes
farther, it is finally dependent upon secondary
factors which are determined by presuppositions
of non-psychological character, and thus the
results may be quite contradictory: the one re-
commends the study of nature, the other only
imagination; the one proposes flowers for models, the other geometrical figures; the one lines,
the other colors. Psychology listens carefully
to all, but is responsible for none of these propositions. An examination of the papers which
drawing-superintendents and drawing-teachers
usually read at their meetings shows, indeed,
that they belong for the most part to a species
well known in all our educational gatherings.
The first half of each paper is made up of famil-

iar sentences taken from good textbooks of physiological psychology, — the ganglion cells of
the optical centres play the chief rôle in the
drawing associations, — and the second half of
the paper contains a list of correct educational
suggestions; only the chief thing, the proof that
the suggestions are really consequences of the
textbook abstracts, is forgotten. The two parts
have often not the slightest connection. The
second half alone would appear commonplace,
and the first alone would appear out of place;
together they make a scholarly impression, even
if they have nothing to do with each other.

Perhaps one other danger in these practical
movements of to-day deserves mention. The
fact that drawings, paintings, pictures, please us,
encourages the working out of technical prescriptions from them for instruction in art; but the
pleasure must be a pure and natural one, as little
as possible dependent upon fugitive fashions and
capricious tastes; and if our pleasure is a refined
eccentricity, or even perversity, it is certain that
we have no right to infect with it the taste of
the younger generation. Seldom has this danger
been so near as in our time, with its preraphael-
itic and Japanese preferences, with its poster style
and its stylistic restlessness. The healthy atmo-
sphere for the taste of the child is harmonious
classical beauty. The man who has passed his
training in pure beauty may reach a point where

a reaction against classicism is a sound and mature æsthetical desire, but to begin with eccentric realism or with mysterious symbolism in an immature age is a blunder. The educational mistake becomes worse if that style is allowed in the schoolroom which is over-indulged in our time, and which is most antagonistic to the child's mind : I mean the primitivistic style of our posters and bindings. The simple forms of primitivistic art are not a real returning to the beginnings of art, which would be quite adapted to children. No; this style means an ironical playing with the primitive forms on the basis of a most artful art. It is masquerading with the costumes of simplicity, not real desire for simple nature; and the spirit of irony alone makes it possible, and so dangerously attractive for our taste. If a school exhibition of drawings in the style of the Yellow Book appears to our eye pleasant and almost refreshing, after the tiresome elaborations of our own school-time, it is our moral duty to ask, not what we like, but what children ought to learn to like. Irony toward the most mature products of civilization ought not to flourish in a child's mind; and if the ironical curves of the Beardsley style become the trained methods of children, who finally believe that they really see nature in conventionalized poster style and use those lines thoughtlessly as patterns, the result is decidedly a perverse one.

Nevertheless, the future may be wiser; psychology will perhaps help pedagogics to find the way to develop the facility of pupils in producing fair drawings; and if we are willing to take the hope for the fact, we may say that psychology gives to the teacher prescriptions for training the child to draw better and better, and, above all, prescriptions which the child itself can learn, prescriptions for the composition and arrangement of a drawing which shall please others. Art can thus be fully described psychologically and explained with regard both to its conditions and to its effects, and both groups of facts can become suggestive for the construction of rules for the teaching of drawing. The relations of psychology and art are then important and suggestive ones; and yet, is that our final word? Has philosophy nothing else to say?

V

I know quite well that there are plenty of men who would say, Yes, that is the whole story. I think, however, the number is increasing of those who see that while half a truth is true as far as its half goes, half a truth is a lie if it pretends to be the whole. It seems to me, indeed, that this psychological scheme is one-sided, and that our time confronts dangers for its ideal life if triumphant psychology crushes under its feet every idealistic opposition. It is with art here exactly as with science and with morality. Psychology proclaims: We can describe and explain every thought of science and every decision of morality from an atomistic naturalistic point of view; we can understand it as the necessary result of the foregoing psychophysical conditions. There is, then, no absolute truth in science, no absolute virtue in morality; duties are trained associations, and the value of our actions, as of our thinking, lies in their agreeable effects. Art easily joins the others; if there is no truth and no virtue which is more than the product of circumstances, then there is no beauty which has absolute value; then beauty has no other meaning than that which psychology describes; it is the effect of certain psychological processes, and the cause of certain agreeable psychological results; and if we are careful to prepare those conditions and to insure that outcome, then we have done all that the æsthetical luxury of society can wish for its entertainment.

I do not deny the right of psychology to consider the world of beautiful creations from such a point of view, and as a psychologist I do my best to help in such investigations; but I cannot forget that this view-point is an artificial one for living, real art; that it is artificial both for the subject who creates art and for the subject who enjoys art; that it is artificial wherever art is felt in its full meaning.

I say that psychology has its full right of
way within its own limits; it has limits, however,
and they are much narrower than the superficial
impression may make us believe. Psychology
has to describe and to explain mental life; but
description and explanation are possible only for
objects. Explanation always presupposes description, and the very idea of description presupposes the existence of objects. Psychology
considers mental life, therefore, only in so far as
it can be thought as a series of existing objects,
— objects which exist in consciousness as physical objects exist in space.

We have not to ask here why it is important
for the purposes of life and thought to consider
the mental world as if it were a world of objects.
We are sure that in the primary reality our
inner life does not mean to us such a world of
objects only. Our perceptions and conceptions
may reach us as objects, while our feelings, our
emotions, our judgments, our volitions, do not
come in question with us first as objects which
we passively perceive, but as activities which we
live out, as activities the reality of which cannot
be described and causally explained; it must be
felt and understood and interpreted. In short,
we are not merely passive subjects with a world
of conscious objects; we are willing subjects,
whose acts of will have not less reality in spite
of the fact that they are no objects at all. To

consider the mental world, including feeling and the will, psychologically means an artificial transformation and substitution which may have its value for special purposes, but which leads us away from reality. The reality of the will and feeling and judgment does not belong to the describable world, but to a world which has to be appreciated; it has to be linked, therefore, not by the categories of cause and effect, but by those of meaning and value. And in this world of will relations grows and blossoms and flowers Art.

Let us examine the characteristics of this great network of will attitudes, in which the personality feels itself a willing subject, and acknowledges all other subjects as volitional also. One distinction is of paramount importance: our will may be thought of as an individual attitude, or it may arise with the meaning of an over-individual decision that demands acknowledgment by every subject, and that is willed, therefore, independently of our merely personal desires. It is an act of will which is meant as necessary for every subject, which ought to be acted by everybody: we call it duty. From a purely psychological standpoint, the will thought as object is determined in any case, — the virtuous act as well as the crime, the nonsensical judgment as well as the wise one. From the critical standpoint of reality, the special will decision is necessary if it belongs to the very nature of will, binds every will, not by natural law, but by obligation; and it can be and is unnecessary if it is merely personal arbitrariness.

This doubleness of duty and arbitrariness in our will repeats itself in every division of possible will activities, and there exist four such departments of relations of will to the world, four possibilities of reacting on the world. First, the subject may change the objects of the world by his actions; secondly, may decide for additional supplements to the given objects; thirdly, may transform the objects in his thought so that they form a connection; and fourthly, may transform the objects so that they stand each for itself. If these four possible subjective acts are performed by the individual personal arbitrary will, they represent individual values. The actions toward the world are then such changes of the objects as are useful and practical for our comfort; the supplementations are then the play of our fancy and imagination; the connections are then expressions of our hope or fear; the isolations, finally, are means to our personal enjoyment. These four functions may be carried out also as functions of the deeper, over-individual, necessary will; that is, as functions of duty. Those actions which alter and change the objective world are then moral actions; the ideas which supplement the world make up religion; those transformations which bring out a connection between the objects of the world compose scientific truth; and finally, those transformations which isolate the objects, so that they stand each for itself, form the domain of beauty.

VI

Truth and beauty thus represent duties, logical and æsthetical duties, just as morality represents ethical duties.   We choose and form the physical axiom in science so, and not otherwise, because our will is bound by duty to do so; that is, only that particular decision of our affirming will can demand acknowledgment by every subject; and thus art chooses the forms and lines, the colors and curves, of the Sistine Madonna just so, and not otherwise, because only this decision of the creating will is as it ought to be, as duty prescribes, as it can demand that every willing subject ought to acknowledge it.   Everything in this world is beautiful, and is a joy forever if it is so transformed that it does not suggest anything else than itself, that it contains all elements for the fulfillment of the whole in itself.   We do not ask for the arms and legs of the person whose marble bust the artist gives us, and we do not ask for his complexion, either. We do not ask how the field and forest look outside of the frame of the landscape painting, and we do not ask what the persons in the drama have done before and will do after the story. Our works of art are not in our space and not in our time; their frame is their own world, which they never transcend. Real art makes us forget that the painting is only a piece of canvas, and that Hamlet is only an actor, and not the prince. We forget the connections, we abstract from all relations, we think of the object in itself; and wherever we do so, we proceed æsthetically. And if we enjoy the great works of art, the essential function is not the individual enjoyment of our senses and feelings, like the enjoyment in eating and drinking; no, it is the volitional acknowledgment of the will of the artist. We will with him; and if we appreciate his work as beautiful, we acknowledge that it is as we feel that it ought to be; that our will of thinking that particle of the world is lifted to its duties; that we have transcended the sphere of merely personal arbitrariness and its desires and agreeable fulfillments; that we have reached the sphere of over-individual values. Whoever understands art as will function believes in art and appreciates it as a world of duties; psychology has not to try to understand it as such, but to transform it into something else, into a set of objects which have causes and effects. Psychology must destroy the deepest meaning of art, just as it disregards the deepest meaning of truth and morality, if it tries to present its view as the last word about our inner activities.

And if art is thus a realization of duties which have their real meaning in this acknowledgment of the will, in what light should we see all these technical rules and prescriptions for facilitating in the child the production of artistic works, and for preventing him from making disagreeable drawings? Those rules and prescriptions remain quite good and valid. They do for real beauty and art just what the police and the prisons on the one side, the training of habits and manners on the other side, do for real morality. Nobody will underestimate the value of the fact that our children learn through training a thousand habits which keep them, as a matter of course, out of conflict with the laws, and that police and jails remind them again and again, Do not leave the safe tracks. Whoever lives a noble life, however, means by morality and duty something else and something higher. Habits and jails do not insure that in an important conflict of life, where personal interests stand against duty, the bad action may not triumph. Only a conscience which is penetrated by morality stands safe in all storms, and such a conscience is not brought out by technical prescriptions, nor by punishments and jails; no, only by the obligatory power of will upon will, by the inspiring life of subjects we acknowledge, by the example of the heroes of duty, that speaks directly from will to will, and for which we cannot substitute psychological training and police officers. And thus the duty of art. Do not believe that the easier production of a not disagreeable drawing means a positive gain for real art and beauty: it raises the standard, it uplifts the level of æsthetic production, just as the standard of moral behavior is lifted by the existence of a watchful police, and it is extremely important. Do not forget, however, that æsthetical life also needs not only the policeman's function, but above all the minister's and helper's function; in other words, not technical rules, but duties; not easy production, but convictions; not knowledge of psychological effects, but belief in absolute values.

This attitude becomes the more important as this whole view shows that the world of art is in no way subordinate to or less true than the world of science. The reality is neither that which the scientist describes nor that which the artist sketches; both are transformations for a special purpose. The scientist, we have seen, transforms for the purpose of connection, and in that service he constructs atoms which exist nowhere but in his thought. The artist transforms in the interest of isolation, and in that service he constructs his drawings. The mechanical process of drawing as such is, of course, not art in itself; it is the indifferent means of expression

which can communicate science as well as art.
Just as words can serve Shakespeare as well as
Darwin, so lines and curves can serve the mathe-
matician and the physicist as well as the artist;
the purpose alone separates the poet from the
biologist, the scientist from the artist.   And if
art thus means a world which is exactly as true
and valuable as the world of science, let us not
forget that the school lesson in drawing means
contact with this world of art, — that is, with
the special spirit of æsthetic duties; and that
every drawing-teacher ought to be, not an
æsthetical policeman only, but an inspiring believer in these sacred æsthetic duties.

PSYCHOLOGY AND HISTORY

I

A STUDY of the relations between psychology and the science of history emphasizes necessarily the limits of psychology. I know quite well that the choice of such a subject easily suggests the suspicion of heresy; whoever asks eagerly for the limits of a science appears to the first glance in a hostile attitude towards it. To emphasize its limiting boundaries means to restrain its rights and to lessen its freedom. It seems, indeed, almost an anti-psychological undertaking for any one to say to this young science, which is so full of the spirit of enterprise: Keep within the bounds of your domain. But you remember the word of Kant: "It is not augmentation, but deformation of the sciences, if we efface their limits." Kant is speaking of logic, but at present his word seems to be for no field truer than for psychology. Psychology, it seems to me, encouraged by its quick triumphs over its old-fashioned metaphysical rival, to-day moves instinctively towards an expansionistic policy. A psychological imperialism which dictates laws

to the whole world of inner experience seems
often to be the goal. But sciences are not like
the domiciles of nations; their limits cannot be
changed by mere agreement. The presuppositions with which a science starts decide for all
time as to the possibilities of its outer extension.
The botanists may resolve to-morrow that from
now on they will study the movements of the
stars also; it is their private matter to choose
whether they want to be botanists only or also
astronomers, but they can never decide that
astronomy shall become in future a part of
botany, supposing that they do not claim the
Milky Way as a big vegetable. Every extension beyond the sharp limits which are determined by the logical presuppositions can thus be
only the triumph of confusion, and the ultimate
arbitration, which is the function of epistemology, must always decide against it. It is
thus love and devotion for psychology which
demands that its energies be not wasted by the
hopeless task of transgressions into other fields.

Philosophers and psychologists are mostly willing to acknowledge such a discriminative attitude when the relations between psychology and
the normative sciences, ethics, logic, æsthetics, are
in question. They know that a mere description and causal explanation of ethical, æsthetical,
and logical mental facts in spite of its legitimate
relative value cannot in itself be substituted for

the doctrines of obligation. The line of demarcation thus separates with entire logical sharpness the duties from the facts, the duties which
have to be appreciated in their validity as ideals
for the will, and the facts which have to be
analyzed and explained in their physical or psychical existence as objects of perception. But
can we overlook the symptoms of growing opposition against the undiscriminative treatment of
the world of facts in the empirical sciences?
The creed of those who believe in such uniformity is simple enough : the universe is made
up of physical and psychical processes, and it
is the purpose of science to discover their elements and their laws ; we may differentiate and
classify the sciences with regard to the different
objects which we analyze or with regard to the
different processes the laws of which we study,
but there cannot exist in the world anything
which does not find a suitable place in a system
in which all special sciences are departments of
physics or of psychology. In a period of naturalistic thinking like that of the Darwinistic age
the intellectual conscience may be fascinated and
hypnotized by the triumphs of such atomizing
and law-seeking thought even to the point of
forgetting all doubts and contradictions. But
the pendulum of civilization begins to swing in
the other direction. The mere decomposition of
the world has not satisfied the deep demand for

an inner understanding of the world; the discovery of the causal laws has not stilled the thirst for emotional values, and there has come a chill with the feeling that all the technical improvement which surrounds us is a luxury which does not make life either better or worthier of the struggle. The idealistic impulses have come to a new life everywhere in art and science and politics and society and religion; historical and philosophical thinking has revived and rushes to the foreground. We begin to remember again what naturalism too easily forgets, that the interests of life have not to do with causes and effects, but with purposes and means, that in life we feel ourselves as units and as free agents, bound by culture and not only by nature, factors in a system of history and not only atoms in a mechanism.

Such a general reaction demands its expression in the world of science too, and there cannot be any surprise if psychology has to stand the first attack. The naturalistic study of the physical facts may not be less antagonistic to such idealistic demands, and yet it is the decomposition of the psychical facts which oppresses us most immediately in our instinctive strife for the rights of the personality. The antithesis becomes thus most pointed in the conflict between psychology and history, and it seems to me that only two possibilities are open.

One possibility is that these sciences stay yoked together, the one forcing the other to follow its path. Either of two events may then happen. Either psychology will remain as hitherto the stronger one; in which case history must follow the paths of psychological analysis and be satisfied with sociological laws; every effort of history which goes beyond that is then unscientific, and the works of our great historians must seek shelter under the roof of art. Or — and this second case has all odds in favor of it — the belief in the unity of personality will become stronger than the confidence in science, which merely decomposes, and psychology will be subordinated to the historical view of man. That is possible under a hundred forms, but the final result must always be the same, the ruin of real psychology. I think this undermining of psychology with the tools of history is to-day in eager progress. Here belong, of course, all the most modern attempts to supplement the regular analyzing psychology by a pseudo-psychology which by principle considers the mental life as a unity and asks not about its constitution but about its meaning. Whether authors, half unconsciously, alternate with these two views from chapter to chapter, or whether they demand systematically that both kinds of psychology be acknowledged, makes no essential difference. Both forms are characteristic for a period of transition; both must lead in the end to giving up fully the analyzing view, to shifting the results of such analysis over to physiology, and thus to confining psychology entirely to the anti-causal categories, that is, to denying psychology altogether. Such turnings of the scientific spirit are slow, but if history and psychology remain chained up together, the symptoms of the future are too clear: there is no hope for psychology.

But there is a second alternative open. The chain which forces psychology and history to move together may be broken; the one may be acknowledged as fully independent of the other. What appears as a conflict of contradictory statements may then become the mutual supplementation of two partial truths, just as a body may appear very different from the geometrical, from the physical, and from the chemical points of view, while each one gives us truth. To those who have followed the recent development of epistemological discussion, especially in Germany, it is a well-known fact that this logical separation of history and psychology is, indeed, the demand of some of the best students of logic. They claim that the scientific interest in the facts can and must take two absolutely different directions: we are interested either in the single fact as such or in the laws under which it stands, and thus we have two groups of sciences which have nothing to do with each other, sciences which describe the isolated facts and sciences which seek their laws. A leading logician baptizes the first, therefore, idiographic sciences, the latter nomothetic sciences; idiographic is history; nomothetic are physics and psychology. Psychology gives general facts which are always true, but concerning which it has not to ask whether they are realized anywhere or at any time; history refers to the special single fact only, without any relation to general facts.

II

I consider this logical separation as a liberating deed, not only because it is the only way for psychology to escape its ruin through the interference of an historically thinking idealism, and also not only because the value and unity and freedom of the personality which history preaches can now be followed up without interference on the part of psychology, but because, independent of any practical results, it seems to me the necessary outcome of epistemological reflection. And yet the arguments which have led to this separation appear to me mistaken and untenable in every respect. I agree heartily with the decision, but I absolutely reject the motives. No antithesis is possible between sciences which study the isolated facts and sciences which generalize; such a methodological difference does not exist. We shall see that it must be replaced by a difference of another kind, but the end must be the same: psychology and history must never come together again. To criticise the one way of attaining this end and to illuminate the other new way which I propose is the purpose of the following considerations.

We must proceed at first critically; what is the truth of the view which contrasts idiographic and nomothetic sciences? At the first glance the importance of the discrimination seems so evident that it appears hard to understand how it could ever have been overlooked. It seems a matter of course that the empirical sciences can ask either about the general facts of reality, the laws which are true always and everywhere and which do not say what happened on a special place and in a special time, or on the other hand about the single facts which are characterized just by their uniqueness. We may be interested in the physical and chemical laws of fire, but our interest in the one great fire which destroyed Moscow has an absolutely different logical source, and if we extend our historical interest from the physical to the psychical side, and investigate the stream of associations which passed through the mind of Napoleon during the days of that fire, we have again an absolutely different kind of interest from that of the psychologist who studies the laws of association

and inhibition, which are true for every mortal.
How small from a logical standpoint appears the
difference between the search for physical laws
and the search for psychological laws compared
with the unbridgable chasm between the search
for laws and the inquiry for special facts which
happened once! And this difference grows if
we consider that all our feelings and emotions
refer to the special single object, not to any
laws, that, above all, the personalities with which
we come in contact come in question for us just
in their singleness, and that we ourselves feel
the value of our life and the meaning of our
responsibility in the uniqueness of the acts by
which we mark our individual rôle in the history of mankind. These arguments of recent
epistemological discussions will easily find the
ear of the multitude. Common sense, which
demands for itself the prerogative of being inconsistent, will probably hesitate only at the
unavoidable postulate of this standpoint, that
also the development of our solar system, of our
earth, of our flora and fauna, belongs then to
history and not to natural science, as they describe a process which happened once, and not
a law.

I may begin my criticism at the periphery of
the subject, moving slowly to the centre. I
claim first that all natural sciences, of which
psychology is one, do not seek laws only, but set

forth also judgments about the existence of objects. Of course, we can make the arbitrary decision that we acknowledge the natural sciences as such only so far as they give eternal laws without reference to their realization in a special place or in a special time, while any judgment about the existence here or there, now or then, has to be housed under the roof of history. The sciences as they practically are would then be mixtures of historical and naturalistic statements, the historical factor diminishing the more, the more abstract the science, reaching its minimum in pure mechanics. Such decision has only recently found able defense, but do we not destroy, by its acceptance, the whole meaning of natural science? Are the laws for themselves alone still of any scientific interest at all? Why do we care at all for such general laws, as the law of causality, the most general of them, which embraces all the others, is included already in the presuppositions of science, and thus anticipated beforehand? When formal logic or mathematics deals with A and B and C, they state valid relations without asking whether A, B or C is given anywhere or at any time, even without excluding the possibility that their real existence may be impossible. The scientific judgments of physics and psychology, on the other hand, have lost all their meaning if we deprive them of the presupposition that objects which prove the validity of such laws have real existence in the world of experience.

We can construct well-founded physiological laws also for the organism of the centaur and psychological laws for the minds of nixes and water fairies, but neither attempt belongs within the system of science. The claim of existentiality is not explicitly expressed in the formulation of scientific knowledge, not because it is unessential, but because it is a matter of course. The larger the circle for which the law is valid, the more we find these included judgments of reality deprived of their reference to special local and temporal data, but even in the most general propositions of mechanics such judgments are tacitly included. The question is not whether the objects with which the laws of mechanics deal have real existence from a philosophical point of view; certainly they have not. The important point is that mechanics by its laws tries at the same time to make us believe that even the atoms have existence. On the other hand, the existential judgment must become the more detailed the more special the law is, that is, the more complicated the conditions of its realization. If the psychologist states the laws of the feelings, he claims that it is not true that only men without feelings exist; he claims that men with feelings have reality too. If he gives us the more special laws of ethical feelings,

he claims that experience knows men with ethical emotion.   If he goes on with his specializa-
tion of the psychical laws, claiming that under
special conditions the ethical emotion of obedience to the state comes to inhibit the desire for
life, he tells us that this really happened.   His
psychological law becomes finally only still more
detailed if he lays it down that under such and
such conditions obedience to the state discharges
itself in′ the drinking of a hemlock potion in
spite of antagonistic suggestions of escape from
philosophical friends.   It is a psychological law,
and yet it claims at the same time that all this
once at least really happened, while the complication of conditions practically excludes the
possibility of its happening more than once in
the world of our experience.

Of course, it remains a law of general character with regard to absolute space and absolute
time; when all conditions including our solar
system and all the events on the earth are given
once more in infinity, then Socrates necessarily
must drink once more the poisoned cup.   But
in the limited space and time of our experience
the conditions for the realization of such a psychological law can have been given only once,
and that they really once were given is decidedly
claimed and thus silently reported by the law.
If our opponents maintain that the naturalistic
sciences need as supplement an historical descrip-

tion of one special stage of the world to give a foothold for the working of the eternal laws, we can thus reject this external help for the explanation of the world, as the laws themselves furnish all that we need. The system of the laws is at the same time a full and graduated system of existential propositions with regard to the limited space and time of our experience. If ever and anywhere in the empirical universe a molecule had moved otherwise or another thought had passed through a consciousness, then the system of laws, thought in ideal perfection, would have demanded a change. Our physics and psychology presuppose and assert the real existence of exactly our world. They do not seek the laws with the intention of neglecting and ignoring the special facts.

III

The separation of the single facts from the general facts is thus untenable, because the explanatory law includes the description; but we can also emphasize the other side of this mutual relation : every description includes explanation, every assertion of a special fact demands reference to the general facts. A description has a logical value only if it points towards a law. We describe a process by the help of conceptions which are worked up from the general facts, common to a group of objects, and these general conceptions are the more valuable for the purposes of description the more their content is a condensed representation of real objective connections.   Descriptions in popular language make use of conceptions which are deduced from superficial similarity, but every new insight into physical and psychological laws gives to these general conceptions a more and more valuable shape.   The history of science is the steady development of the means of description; there is no description which by its use of conceptions does not aim at working out the laws.   Thus, far from the trivial belief that the law is merely a description of facts, we ought not to forget that the description of facts involves the laws and is only another form of their expression. To describe a physical thing as a group of atoms or an idea as a group of sensations demands the whole knowledge of the psychological and mechanical laws and condenses in its conceptions the progress of science.   To separate the descriptive report from the explaining apperception is thus again impossible.

It might appear that this does not hold for all kinds of description; we communicate with one another in practical life without relying on general conceptions.   But our communication then is no description.   Any mode of personal expression, gestures or tears, may tell us what is going on in the mind of another without reference to psychological laws. But the fact is that they give no description either; they give a suggestion. The words of practical life, the words of the poet, and, as we may add at once, the words of the historian, work like such movements of expression; they make every mental vibration resound in us, because they force us unintentionally or with conscious art to follow the suggestion and to imitate the mental experience. The rhythm and the shade of the words may then be substituted for logical exactitude, and interjections may have deeper influence than complete judgments, but all that is decidedly no description, as a description demands a communication of the elements. Such a suggestion allows us an understanding of the meaning, but gives us no knowledge of the constitution. Where a single object really has to be described, there conceptions and laws are inevitable, and the historian cannot make an exception.

But just this fact, that description and explanation cannot be separated and that the conception includes the law, has opened in recent philosophical discussions a new way of thought which also seems to lead to those claims which we rejected. Granted, it is said, that every description presupposes generalizing abstractions, but such abstraction must then lead us away from the endless manifoldness of the reality. Every scientific description deals with physical or psychological abstractions; does that not mean that we need still another kind of treatment which does justice to the existing richness and fullness of the real single fact? If we give this mission to history, we acknowledge that its communications would not be ordinary descriptions, but in any case we should again have the separated camps with the antithesis: Manifoldness and abstraction, single fact and general fact. But the presupposition is wrong; the manifoldness of the reality is not endless and the abstracting conceptions are not at all unfit to do justice to the richness of the single fact. The single conception abstracts, but the connection of conceptions in the sentence reconstructs again. On the other hand, whatever is the possible object of perception and discrimination must be the possible object of descriptive determination. Whether the task of a complete conceptional description is difficult or not is no question of principle; impossible it is not. The ability to perceive differences is even inferior compared with the power to separate the differences conceptionally, and the abstracting description of science must, therefore, frequently increase and not decrease the manifoldness of the object. We know about the objects more than we perceive; above all, the description can never leave behind it a perceivable remainder which from its too great manifoldness excludes description. The full variety of the single facts thus belongs just as much as the most general law to the physical and psychological sciences; the antithesis psychology and history as coinciding with the antithesis abstraction and manifoldness of reality is then impossible. That history stands, indeed, nearer to reality than any psychology we shall later fully acknowledge, but, as we shall see, for very different reasons; history abstracts, we shall see, not less than psychology, and psychology is interested in the variety of the facts just as much as is history.

IV

This brings us to our central arguments: Every science considers the single facts in their relations to other facts, works towards connection, towards generalities. Science means connection and nothing else, and history also aims at general facts, or it cannot hope for a place in the system of science. Does that mean that it is valueless to consider the single fact as it stands for itself, isolated and separated from everything else? Certainly not; the isolation is not less valuable than the connection, but it never forms a science; it is the task of art. The single fact belongs to art and not to history; history has to do with the general facts. That is the thesis which I must interpret and defend. One point, of course, is clear before the discussion. If we maintain that history has also to work up its material with respect to the general facts and not with regard to the single facts, then it is evident that there is in the deepest principle of the inquiry no methodological difference between physics and psychology on the one side and history on the other.   But we insisted that an important difference does exist.   The difference must then be not in the kind of treatment, but in the material itself.   To be sure, there cannot be a physical or psychical object in the universe which would not be possible material for psychology or physics; if history deals with a material which is different from the possible objects of those empirical sciences, then it must deal with facts which differ from the physical and psychical objects in their kind of existence; in short, the difference between psychology and history is not a methodological but an ontological one.

We must then ask what kind of existence belongs to the material with which physics and psychology deal, and how it is related to reality; above all, how far reality offers still another kind of facts which could be the substance of other sciences.   Reality means to us here the immediate experience which we live through. This immediate truth of life may be transformed and remoulded in theories and sciences, and these remodelings of reality may be highly valuable for special purposes of life; we may even reach finally a point of reconstruction from which the subjective experience appears as an illusion and the supplementation stands as the only truth. Yet the importance of such constructions must not make us forget that we have then left reality behind us. Our doubting and remoulding itself belongs to the reality for which its products can never be substituted. And this primary reality can, of course, never be reached when we start from the finished theories of the physical or psychological sciences. Whether we pretend that the world is a content of our consciousness, a system of psychological ideas, or whether we start from the mechanical universe and consider experience as effect of the outer world on the consciousness, or whether we confuse the two and call the world a product of the brain, it is all equally misleading if we seek the reality, as each view presupposes equally the psychological or physical constructions. It is then, of course, also impossible for us to reach the less remoulded primary experience by going backward through the genetic development of the individual or of the race to an earlier simpler stage of experience. Just this genetic tracing backward fully presupposes the categories of the psychological view; we must have already considered our own inner life as a complex combination of elements before it has a meaning to call the mental life of the child or of the animal less complex; the starting point of the genetic development is thus itself an artificial construction which lies further away from the primary experience.

If we thus escape all theories and stand firm against the suggestions which psychology and physics plentifully bring to us, then we find in the reality nothing of ideas or of mechanical substances, neither consciousness nor a connected universe. The reality we experience does not know the antithesis of psychical and physical objects, but in the primary stage merely the antithesis subject and object. We feel our personal reality in our subjective attitudes, in our will acts which we do not perceive but which we live through, and with the same immediacy we acknowledge other personalities as subjects of will. They too are not objects which we merely perceive, but we acknowledge them, by our feeling, as subjects with whom we agree or disagree and whose reality is thus not less certain than our own. Our acts as subjects are directed towards objects which in reality exist only as such objects of will, that is, as values. They are our ends and means, our tools and purposes, and nothing is to us real that is not called to be selected or rejected, to be favored or dismissed. Subjective acts of will and objects of will form the reality, the whole reality, nothing

lies outside, and nothing is valid beyond this
world of will relations; and even if we form
judgments about objects which we think as
independent of the will, this judgment and this
thought itself is an act of will working towards
a purpose.

As soon as we begin to bring order into the
manifoldness of this real world, the subjective
acts as well as the objects divide themselves into
two groups, — those of individual character and
those which are common to all, over-individual.
This division is not a result of counting whether
several subjects or by chance only one subject
have made the decision or appreciated the object:
it is a question of intention merely. My act is
over-individual if it is willed with the meaning
that it belongs to every subject which I acknowledge, and my object is over-individual in so far
as I consider it as a possible object of attitude
for every subject. My over-individual will-act is
that factor of reality which we call duty; every
duty lies in us as subjects, as our own deepest
will, and yet as more than our individual decision. The over-individual objects are those
which we call physical; the individual objects
are the psychical ones; we must only not forget that these physical and psychical objects
are in reality not in question as independent objects of perception, but are always related to the
will; they are not contents of consciousness and

mechanical bodies in a continuous space, but suggestions which have a meaning, things which have a use. We find thus four factors of reality, beyond whose validity a constructive metaphysics alone can go. Metaphysics may ask whether the individual and over-individual acts do not blend in an absolute subject and whether the objects are not posited by such a subject of higher order; epistemology must be satisfied with the more modest task of settling how we deal with this reality in our scientific or æsthetic knowledge. Reality itself is, of course, neither art nor science, but life. Art and science must be thus transformations of the material which life offers to us, while these transformations themselves are acts of the subjects and thus belonging to those will-formations which claim for themselves an over-individual character, creating the values of beauty and truth.

V

The acts which lead from life to art and science are thus for epistemology free acts of that subjectivity which we find in ourselves by immediate feeling, and which we acknowledge in others by an understanding of their propositions and suggestions; they are not functions of the psychophysical organism, not psychophysical processes, as we must have reached already the artificial reconstruction of science before the subject is replaced by that object among other objects, the psychophysical personality. Scientific and æsthetic acts are not the only functions of the real subject; the ethical and others stand coördinated, but we are concerned here only with the two functions which do not aim to change and to improve the world, but to rethink it in beautiful or truthful creations. It seems to me now that the two attitudes are in every respect antagonistic; to express their direction in a short formula, I should say science connects the factors of reality; art, on the other hand, isolates them. The material of science and of art is then the same, though treated by a different method. Both can deal with all the four factors of reality, with individual acts and over-individual acts, with individual objects and over-individual objects. Life does not isolate fully, and gives no complete connection; whatever we turn to with our will has features which lead us further and further to ever new interests; life does not let us sink into the one alone — we rush beyond it to new realities. And life does not give connections beyond the immediate needs of practical purposes in the narrow circle of chance experience. Wherever is full isolation of single facts there is beauty, wherever truth there must be full connection.

The assertion that every isolated fact in its singleness means beauty has for us here only

the character of a critical argument and is not
for itself an object of our discussion. It has for
us merely the negative purpose of proving that
the singleness cannot be characteristic of history. We cannot here defend this assertion by
detailed discussion; we have only to elucidate
its meaning. Certainly the real life, too, brings
us pulses of experience in which our will is cap-
tivated by the given experience, satisfied with
the object in itself or in the acknowledgment of
other subjective acts; then we have the beauty
of nature, the beauty of forms and of landscapes, of love and of friendship. Of course,
it is only an exception when life offers to us in
the untransformed reality such complete beauty;
it remains the duty of art to change the world
till everything is eliminated that leads the subject beyond the single experience, and the will
can rest in the single fact. The world of objects is thus transformed in painting and sculpture, the world of subjective acts remoulded in
poetry. The sentiment or the conflict which
the poet suggests to us, the bust or the landscape which the artist brings before our eye, is
severed from the practical world; as long as
anything connects it with the background of the
daily world it may be useful or inspiring or instructive, but it is not beautiful. The poet pro-
jects his work into an ideal past; the painter
cuts an ideal space out of the reality, and the

sculptor fills an ideal space, not the space of our surrounding, to take care thus that the acts and objects may not link into our real world, may never become causes for outer effects, motives for actions, or centres for associations which lie beyond the frame.

We ought not to become skeptical in regard to this point on account of the overhasty generalizations in which empirical psychology mostly characterizes the æsthetic act as rich in associations. The epistemological problem we are discussing cannot be settled by psychology, yet as soon as the facts are expressed in the terms of psychological language they cannot possibly assert the opposite of the epistemological truth. But there is no reason for such a conflict, as psychology is undoubtedly in the wrong. The psychological claim is based on the general theory that all pleasant mental states represent an increase of activity, and with it an increase of associations, while all unpleasant states are marked by a decrease of activity and lack of associations. I think that is wrong; there are different kinds of increase and different kinds of decrease in both ideas and actions. The antithesis pleasure and displeasure does not at all coincide with increase and decrease if we do not arbitrarily select such emotions as joy on the one and grief on the other side. Increase of activity characterizes pleasant and unpleasant states, only in the pleasant states it produces action of the extensors, in the unpleasant states action of the flexors. In the same way decrease of activity can have a double type: it can have its ground in the absence of stimulations, and this is, indeed, characteristic of some unpleasant states; but the lack of outer action can have its ground also in the fact that every motor impulse goes to the antagonistic muscles equally. This increase of tonicity without possible action is characteristic for one pleasant state above all, the æsthetic one. The increase and decrease of associations is here, as always, parallel with the motor impulses. Here also increase of associations is essential for some pleasant states, but for some unpleasant ones too, only, like muscle activity, it is in antagonistic directions, in the one case turning to the future, in the other case falling back to the past. And the same doubleness is to be noted in the decrease of associations; in some unpleasant states the decrease comes from a mere lack of ideational impulses, in some pleasant states from the fascination which leads every ideational impulse again to the object itself, so that no thought can lead beyond it. This is again true, above all, for the æsthetic state. The beautiful object includes all that it suggests in itself, and where we connect we sin against the spirit of beauty.

VI

By the contrast with art the fullest light falls on the process of science; every step towards science leads in the opposite direction. The incomplete connections of life are severed by art, but made complete by science, while the material is the same. We had four groups of facts in reality, and we must thus have four groups of sciences which bring systematic connections into the four different fields. We have the science of the over-individual objects, that is, physics; secondly, the science of the individual objects, that is, psychology; thirdly, the sciences of the over-individual will-acts, that is, the normative sciences; and last, not least, the sciences of the individual will-acts, that is, the historical sciences. Physics and psychology have thus to do with objects; history and the normative systems, ethics, logic, æsthetics, deal with will-acts. Psychology and history have thus absolutely different material; the one can never deal with the substance of the other, and thus they are separated by a chasm, but their method is the same. Both connect their material; both consider the single experience under the point of view of the totality, working from the special facts towards the general facts, from the experience towards the system. And yet the difference of material must, in spite of the equality of the methodological process, produce absolutely different kinds of systems of science. We must consider again from the standpoint of real life how the connection of objects is different from the connection of attitudes, and how the purposes of the systematizing reconstruction are different in the two cases.

We and the other subjects have objects which are in reality, as we have seen, objects of our will. Why have we an interest in considering the objects from a scientific standpoint, that is, in systematized connection? If we do so, it must serve, of course, a special purpose in our real life. The purpose is clear. We cannot do the duties of our life, that is, we cannot act on the objects, if we do not know what to expect from them with regard to the reality which we prepare, and we call the reality which we can still prepare the future. We must ask, therefore, what we have to expect for the future from the objects alone, that is, from the objects thought as if they were independent from the subjective will reaction. The answer to this question as to our justified expectations is the system of physical and psychological sciences. To reach this end we must think the objects, the individual or over-individual ones, as if they were no longer objects of a will, as if the subject were deprived of its real activity and were a merely passive perceiving subject the objects of which are thus

definitely cut away from the will. Our interest
was to determine their influence on the future.
We thus consider every object as the cause of
an expected effect, and call those characteristics
of the object which determine our expectation of
the effect its elements. Physics and psychology
thus look on their objects as complexes of elements. It is the task of science to reconstruct
and to transform the objects till each is conceived as such a combination of elements that
the effects to be expected can be fully determined from the elements. In this service grew
up the atom doctrine in physics and the sensation doctrine in psychology. Each object is
thus linked into a causal system; each is considered not as that which it really is, but as a
complex of constructed factors which are substituted for the purpose of the causal connection,
and each is in question in its relation to all the
others. The world thus becomes a system of
causally linked objects which can be described
by their elements, while these elements themselves are chosen from the point of view of
explanation by causality. The determination of
the effects by means of the elementary causes is
expressed by the laws which give the rules for
our expectations. We can say thus that physics
and psychology may very well consider any special facts, and, as we have seen, they certainly
do not ignore the special facts at all, but they

consider them with regard to the causal law, and the laws as types of causal connections are thus the only general facts towards which the systematized study of objects can lead us.

Quite different is the systematic connection of the subjective will-attitudes; we may abstract here at first from the over-individual attitudes and concentrate our interest on the individual will-acts. In psychology the will-attitude as such, as act of the real subject, cannot have any place whatever; psychology deals with objects; the subjective attitude is never an object; it is never perceived; it is experienced by immediate feeling and must be understood and interpreted, but not described and explained. If psychology wishes to treat of the will, the psychophysical organism must be substituted for the real subject, and thus the will be considered as a process in the world of objects. The description of any known will-acts as psychophysical functions, that is, as illustrations of psychological laws, thus as a matter of course belongs to psychology, and if the psychologist should analyze into psychophysical elements and explain as causally determined all will-acts and human functions of the last three thousand years, he would not transcend the limits of psychology. It would be a very useless psychological undertaking, but it would be such and not history. History starts from and deals with the real subjective will-acts which cannot be found in the world of psycho-physical objects.

Our personal life in its political, economical, religious, scientific, æsthetic, technical, and practical aspects is a manifoldness of will-attitudes and acknowledgments. We live in the midst of a variety of political and social, technical and practical institutions, but no institution means anything else than expectations and demands which reach our will, and suggestions towards which we take attitudes. State and church, legal community and social set, what else are they but will-attitudes which we acknowledge and which are, therefore, never understood in their real meaning if they are considered as describable objects, but which must be interpreted and appreciated as subjective will-relations, striving towards purposes and ends. And to understand all the technical and practical institutions which civilization brings to us means again not to describe or explain them, but to interpret them as will-suggestions to be imitated. The machine and the book, the law and the poem, are not physical and psychical objects for our interests as living men, but suggestions and demands for the understanding of the intentions and attitudes of other subjects which we can enter into only by taking an imitating or rejecting attitude, thus reaching will by will. All our knowing and believing, our enjoying and respecting — as long as we abstract from their over-individual values — all our education and civilization, our politics and our professional work, is such a complex of real affirmations and negations, demands and inhibitions, agreements and disagreements, which have to be understood and felt and interpreted, but which are not touched in their reality if merely their psycho-physical substitutions are analyzed and causally explained.   To be a Chinese or a Mohammedan, a symbolist or an Hegelian or an atomist, means to be the subject of special complexes of will-attitudes and nothing else.   If, for instance, we substitute the race for the state, then, of course, we have objects before us and no longer subjective attitudes, but then we deal with biological conceptions and no longer with history.

VII

The manifoldness of will-acts the totality of which forms my real personality thus refers in every act to the will acts and attitudes of other subjects which I acknowledge or oppose, imitate or overcome.   These demands and suggestions of others are not in question in my life as causes or partial causes of my will; they have not to be sought in the interest of a causal connection; they are merely conditions which I as subject of attitude and acts presuppose for my free decision, and which are thus logically contained in it; the

connection is, therefore, not a causal, but merely
a teleological one.   The endless world of will-
acts which stands thus in teleologically determining relation to our own will-attitudes forms the
only material of history.

The material is, of course, unlimited.   If
every act of ours means an attitude towards acts
of others which we must try to understand, it
is clear that those others are understood only
if their acts again are interpreted as attitudes
towards the propositions and demands and suggestions of others, and so on and on.   Every
will-act is thus ideally related to an unlimited
manifoldness of other acts, just as the movement
of every grain of sand is causally related to every
molecule in the universe.   It is the unique task
of history as a science to work out and make
complete this teleological system of individual
will-relations, thus to bring out the connections
between our acts and all the acts which we must
acknowledge as somehow teleologically influen-
cing our own.   While physics and psychology
thus produce a connected system of causes and
effects, linking all objects which stand in connection with our objects, history follows up all
the subjective acts which stand in will-relation to
our subjective attitudes.

Physics and psychology, as we have seen,
reach this end through striving towards laws
and causality; that, of course, cannot be the

way of history. The objects interested us only
as factors which influence the future, and the
laws by which we have connected them have
satisfied this expectant interest. The subjects,
on the other hand, do not interest us primarily
as causes of effects. Of course, we are able to
consider them also as objects which produce
effects, and that aspect may become important to
us in many practical respects; psychophysics will
fully satisfy this kind of interest. And in the
same way we may look on the development of
peoples with an interest in what we have to expect from them; they are then sociological organisms, the laws of which we study; but such
study is not history. The aim of the real historian is not to prophesy the future. Peoples
never learn from history, and the forgotten doctrine that we ought to study history to find out
what we have to expect from the future stands
on the same level with its contemporary, the
doctrine that it is the purpose of art to instruct
us and to make us better. No, the historian
makes us understand the system of will-attitudes
to which our individual will is related. That,
indeed, alone, is our primary interest in the will-
acts of other subjects; we want to understand
them, not to analyze them into elements; we
want to interpret their meanings and not to cal-
culate their future. The objects awake our expectations; the subjects interest our appreciation,

and all that we want to know about them is with what other attitudes they agree or disagree. We thus have the logical aim, to consider them in their relations to all other will-attitudes and to work out the system of these connections; that is, to consider the institutions which are the representatives of will-suggestions, together with the personalities themselves, as links of this endless chain of will-relations.

The purpose of history is not reached until every institution and personality with which we may be in a direct or indirect will-relation is understood as a complex of agreements and disa-agreements, that is, of will-attitudes towards other subjects. This regress must be, of course, infinite, just as no physical process can be reached which has not again causes and effects ; and this task demands also, like the naturalistic sciences, a continual transformation. Just as the physical object is not really a complex of atoms and the psychological idea not really a complex of sensations, but must be in thought transformed into such to make causal connection possible, so in exactly the same way history must reconstruct the personalities and institutions as complexes of will-attitudes, which they really are not, but as which they must be considered to make the unbroken teleological connection possible. And, again, like physics and psychology, history too cannot communicate to us the whole of the connected system, but has to work out the general facts which give to every single fact at once its place in the whole system. These general facts in the teleological will-system cannot be causal laws, but must be will-relations of more and more comprehensive character. Just as in the world of objects the general law covers and determines the causal changes of an unlimited number of objects, so the important will-actions cover and determine in the world of subjects the impulses and suggestions for the decisions and attitudes of an unlimited number. The regularity of the causal law and the importance of the imposing will lift in a corresponding way the general fact over the level of the single facts. It is the work of history to make conspicuous the increasingly important will-influences, as it is the work of physics and psychology to work out the laws. If I say I am a German, I want to assert by that statement that I acknowledge by my will a world of laws, institutions, hopes and ideals which are the will-demands of an undetermined multitude of subjects; this multitude constitutes the historical nation of Germany. But it would be unscientific if I should start to interpret the attitude of every one who is part of that chaotic mass of subjects; it is the work of science to find those influences which determined the multitude, those will-acts which were imitated and acknowledged by the

unimportant subjects. The chaos thus becomes
order, and Goethe and Beethoven, Kant and
Hegel, Luther and Bismarck, stand as the general facts for the millions and millions of less
important subjects who were determined by their
suggestions. Any individual's historical place
is then characterized by his will-attitudes towards the leaders. Just as the naturalist knows
a whole hierarchy of sciences which work out
increasingly general laws up to mechanics as the
most abstract system, so history can consider in
different stages the will-relations of more and
more comprehensive character. The most abstract view is represented by the so-called philosophy of history, which aims at understanding
the history of the world as determined by one
decision of the will. In this spirit the conception of original sin in the theological systems of
the Middle Ages was in the field of historical
thinking perhaps not less marvelous than the
conception of atomistic mechanism in the realm
of natural science. The fact that Adam did not
exist in reality is as little an objection to the
mediæval construction as the fact that no atom
can really exist militates against our atomism;
both reconstructions of reality fill merely ideal
places as necessary goals of thought.

On the other hand, in the same way that
mechanics does not lower the importance of
special natural sciences, no all-embracing theory

of the history of man can interfere with the importance of the special historic disciplines down to the biographies of single personalities. But even the biography has to work in the same direction as the most abstract philosophy of history, in the direction of general connection. The real biography written in an historical spirit shows in the individual the attitudes towards the demands and suggestions which make the history of mankind; the single man becomes thus the crossing point of all the political, technical, religious, æsthetical, intellectual impulses of his time, and he is thus by the will-attitudes which constitute his personality connected with the whole universe of will-acts. As the astronomer in his calculations describes the one curve of a star as the combination of a large number of impulses by attraction, and thus brings the star in relation to the whole firmament, so the historical biographer reconstructs the one life as a system of single attitudes towards an endless multitude of demands and suggestions. It is a complete transformation in the service of connection. The man's life can be told otherwise also: the life as he feels it as a personal experience; so also do we learn to understand the man, but we have then poetry and not history; it is isolation and not connection. And if, instead, we describe and explain his life as a set of ideas, feelings, emotions, and volitions which arose in his psychophysical system from birth to death, then we have again a transformation in the service of connection, but this time for the causal connection of objects, not for the teleological connection of subjects; it is again not history, but psychology.

VIII

The separation of the material of the two sciences is thus simple and clear; there can never be a doubt about the line of demarcation, as there is no psychophysical object in the world — from the sensations of a frog up to the ideas of Newton, the emotions of Byron, and the volitions of Cromwell — which is not a suitable object of psychology, and as there is no subjective individual act which cannot be linked into the endless teleological system of history. A division of material, as if a social psychology, for instance, were to deal with the psychical processes of the unknown masses, while history were to deal with the psychical processes of the well-known men, is an absurdity. Not less misleading would be an antithesis between savagery and civilization. From a psychophysical standpoint such a line is secondary; the organism which adds outer appendages to his body to make the psychophysical functions more effective has reached merely a higher stage of biological development, but is not different in prin-

ciple from the lower type in which nature does
not provide for detachable acquisitions of the
organism.　The animal which runs with locomotives, sees with microscopes, hears with tele-
phones, makes gestures of expression through
newspapers, attacks through cannons, and remembers through libraries, stands above the savage as
a dog stands above a jelly-fish, but it is theoretically nothing new; it is a more complicated product of nature which, therefore, offers a more
difficult problem to the descriptions and explanations of psychology and physiology, but does
not as such become material for history.　And
still another line of separation must disappear;
the fight between the "materialists" and the
"idealists" of the recent economical schools has
nothing to do with the doubleness of psychological naturalism and real historical aspect.　If
the materialists claim that every occurrence
among men is the direct or indirect effect of
economical causes, while the idealists consider
other causes still which seem to them independent
of material conditions, for instance, religious
and patriotic emotion or ambition and love, both
sides stand fully on the ground of psychology
and outside of history.　Those emotions of
practical idealism are in question only as psychophysical causes, and are thus material merely for
a causal system.　In the system of history exists
no causality.

Here is the point where even the historians themselves are inclined to compromises which, at least in principle, must be rejected. Whether or not practically quite interesting reports of periods of civilization can be written by mixing the two attitudes is secondary. Historians, we know, produced in earlier times their deepest effects by mixing history with ethics, but the philosopher at least must be clear that ethics is not history, and he ought to be still less in doubt that a causally explaining social psychology is not history either. As soon as it is acknowledged that we have, on the one side, an interest to consider human life as an object and thus to describe and to explain it, and that we have, on the other side, a logical aim to understand human life as subjective acts which can be interpreted and linked together only by will-attitudes, then we must have the energy to keep the two systems separated. Each is logically valuable, each is therefore true, but if confused both become logically useless.

We can say that Socrates remained in the prison because his knee muscles were contracted in a sitting position and not working to effect his escape, and that these muscle-processes took place because certain psychophysical ideas, emotions, and volitions, all composed of elementary sensations, occurred in his brain, and that they, again, were the effects of all the causes which sense stimulations and dispositions, associations and inhibitions, physiological and climatic influences, produced in that organism. And we can say, on the other hand, that Socrates remained in the prison because he decided to be obedient to the laws of Athens unto death. This obedience means, then, not a psychophysical process, but a will-attitude which we must understand by feeling it and living through it, an attitude which we cannot analyze, but which we interpret and appreciate. The first is a psychological description; the second is an historical interpretation. Both are true. They are, to be sure, not equally valuable for science, as that particular psychophysical process is not more important for the understanding of the psychological system than millions of other emotions in unknown men, while that will-attitude influenced by its demand the acknowledging will of twenty centuries, and is thus most important in the historical system. And yet both are equally true, while they blend into an absurdity if we say that those psychophysical states in the brain of Socrates were the objects which inspired the will of his pupils and were suggestive through two thousand years.

A history which interprets subjectively and understands their purposes out of the deeds of men relinquishes, indeed, its only aim if it coördinates these teleological relations with the causal explanation of human happenings from climatic and geographical, technical and economical, physiological and pathological influences. The subject which is determined by purposes is free ; the action which is the effect of causes is unfree. In the unfree world there cannot be any action which must not be understood causally, and we have no right to stop at any point in our explanation ; the unexplained action means only an unsolved problem which is in no way solved if we seek for its subjective meaning instead of its elements and causes. In the world of freedom, on the other hand, it would be meaningless to ask for cause, as the objects then come in question merely as objects for the willing subjects and not as realities for themselves. The realm of freedom is not made up of oases in the world of necessity ; the reality of history is not spread here and there over the field of nature, but lies fully outside of its limits. The antithesis between psychology and history is thus not law and single event, but causality and freedom, and this difference is the logical result of the ontological difference of the material, the one dealing with objects, the other with subjects. Both go methodologically the same way, considering the single facts from the point of view of the general fact, and both transforming the disconnected material until a perfectly connected system is reached. But because objects are understood by describing and explaining them, while subjects are understood by interpreting and appreciating them, the connection of the one system must be causal, that of the other system teleological, and the general fact in the one field must be a law and in the other field the will relation of importance. As every subjective act can be replaced by a psychophysical function of an organism in the world of objects, and as every object can be understood as a value for a will, the whole reality can be brought without any possible remainder under the one aspect as well as under the other. History, in the real historical spirit, then need no longer fear that the progress of psychology can inhibit its functions, and the psychologist need not feel discouraged that his psychological laws of history appear so utterly trivial to the historian. That which is important for psychology, that which is fit for constructing connections between psychological objects, has the privilege of being indifferent for the historian, that is, of being unfit to link subjective will - attitudes. Psychology and history cannot help each other and cannot interfere with each other as long as they consistently stick to their own aims. Each of them has thus unlimited opportunities for development. The processions of the great psychologists from Aristotle to Herbart, and that of the great historians from Thucydides to

Macaulay, can both have for the future an unlimited number of followers without any quarrel,
in spite of the naturalistic claims of our age,
which for a while was under the illusion that all
is understood when all is explained, and that the
historians had better become psychologists.

IX

As soon as the difference of the two stand-
points is recognized, light falls on all the special
characteristics of the two sciences. Now we
understand why history stands so much nearer
to real life than psychology. Not, as it was
suggested, because history deals with single facts
and psychology with general facts, but because
psychology deals with objects which are thought
as independent of the subject, while in reality
and so in history the material is acknowledged
only in relation to willing subjects. In real life
we are subjects which must be understood but
not described; psychology starts thus at once
with a material which in its singleness is already
farther away from reality than the material with
which history deals. Now we understand also
why the substance of history has value for us,
while the objects of psychology and of all naturalistic sciences are emotionally indifferent. That
is not, as it was suggested, because the single
facts are important for us and the general facts
indifferent; no, it is because the psychological

objects, the contents of consciousness, are thought
as cut loose from the will and thus no longer
possible objects for appreciation, while the historical objects are thought as in their relation to
the attitudes of the will. Now we understand
also under which principle the historian selects
his material. If we accept the view that all
single facts belong to history as such, it is arbitrariness to chronicle Napoleon's battles and
state acts but not his flirtations and breakfasts,
while now we understand how it is that this
selection means the most essential part of the
historian's work, as it is the way to transform
the reality into a system of teleological connections, thus dropping more and more the will-acts
which have no teleological importance for will-
attitudes of other subjects. Now we understand
also why the language of the historian has so
much similarity with that of the poet. The historian, we have seen, has aims which are directly
antagonistic to those of the poet, as the poet
isolates, while the historian, like every scientist,
connects his material. But the materials themselves, the subjective acts, are common to the
poet and the historian. Where the psychologist
encourages the reader to take the attitude of the
objectively perceiving observer, the poet and the
historian speak of facts which can be understood
only by interpretation and inner imitation ; they
cannot be described by enumerating their ele-

ments; they must be suggested and reach somehow the willing subject which enters into the
subjective attitude of the other. Thus the means
of both may approximate to each other. The
poet and the historian may use the same methods of suggestion to reinforce in the reader the
subjectifying attitude which is the presupposition
for the understanding of the isolated will-acts in
the work of poetry and the connected will-acts
in the work of history, while the psychologist
has to adapt even his style and his presentation
to the service of his objectifying aim.

But we now understand and see in a new light
also the relations of the psychological and historical sciences to the normative doctrines, to
ethics, logic, and æsthetics. As long as history
appears merely as a part of psychology or as long
as the one is given over to single facts, the other
to laws, all the normative sciences stand without
any inner relation to any empirical science, those
speaking of duties, these of facts. For us the
relation takes a very different form. We have
seen that all the historical sciences are systems
of individual will-relations and nothing else. On
the other hand, we have found that duty never
means anything but our own over-individual will-
act. All the normative sciences are thus the
systematic connections of our over-individual
will-attitudes, our will-attitudes aiming toward
morality and truth and beauty and religion. As

the over-individual will is, of course, thought as independent of the individual subject, the connection which is sought cannot lead as it did in history from subject to subject; as all subjects are presupposed as agreeing in their over-individual acknowledgment, the connection, the scientific aim can then lie here merely in the systematic connection of our own over-individual purposes and their interpretation. Here, too, a transformation becomes necessary in the interest of connection; each single will-attitude must be linked into this teleological system and must thus be transformed till it represents a crossing point of all the ethical, æsthetical, religious, and logical impulses and demands. The normative sciences and history stand thus in the nearest relation to each other; both are transformations of will-acts in the service of teleological connection, only the one reconstructs and systematizes the individual will-acts in us, the other the over-individual will-acts.

The relation between these two groups of sciences, the historical and the normative ones, is thus perfectly parallel to the relation between the psychological sciences and the physical sciences, of which the one systematizes the individual objects and the other the over-individual objects. The proportion — history stands to the normative doctrines as psychology stands to physics — is, indeed, true in every respect and in every consequence. We may consider here as our last word only one of them. The historical development of the naturalistic sciences shows the continuous tendency to take more and more of the properties of the physical object into the psychological object, that is, to show that the apparent over-individual qualities of the thing are qualities which depend upon the individual; color and sound, smell and taste, go over from the physical thing into the idea, and thus the whole manifoldness of our experience moves over into the sphere of ideas. In exactly the same way and led by the same methodological motives, history takes more and more of the normative duties over into its own field, and shows how the special duties, the logical beliefs, ethical convictions, æsthetical demands and religious postulates are the results of individual attitudes under the suggestion of the individual groups of will-influences. The absolute duties and beliefs and obligations and truths seem thus lost in our life as the colors and sounds and smells are lost for the physical objects. But the parallelism holds for the end-point of this development too. We must deprive the physical object of its colors and sounds, but we cannot give up the truth that there is a physical object nevertheless, as the quantitative reality to which we project, with objective truth, our sensations and ideas; all the naturalistic sciences would be destroyed if we were to give up this realistic conviction of physics. In the same way we may take into the individual all the single over-individual special duties of special nations and ages and social groups, but the reality of the background of projection we cannot give up. Whatever history teaches, the postulate of the reality of duties, of absolute values, stands firm. The absolute duties may be abstract and deprived of color and sound as is the world of physics, but they stand and must last like the physical universe, and whoever in striving towards truth denies the reality of absolute values and gives up the belief in morality and the belief in logic, thus destroys and undermines his own endeavor to find the truth as logical thinker and to stand for the truth as ethical man.

PSYCHOLOGY AND MYSTICISM

I

MYSTICISM — that is, the belief in supernatural connections in the physical and psychical worlds — has always been an interesting object of observation for the psychologist. When the human mind believes that it has reached the realm unseen, psychology can analyze its inner experiences and follow up the devious paths from empirical knowledge to the knowing of the mysterious Unknowable. From this point of view, psychology finds a wonderful field of work in the mystical systems from the earliest Hindoo speculation to the spiritualistic doctrines of to-day; and its interest in mysticism is the deeper and more spontaneous, the more complicated the motives which push the soul beyond the limits of natural insight. Religious emotion and hysterical rapture, mysterious fears and superstitious habits, pathological disturbances and surprising experiences, abnormal credulity and dissatisfaction with science, and very many other true and half-true impulses come in question. Even the pseudo-mystic, who deceives the world because he knows that the world wishes to be deceived, becomes an attractive object for psychological analysis; fanaticism regarding the church and greed for bread and butter, hysterical pleasure in irritating tricks and sensuous pleasure in power over others, are here among the most characteristic features. What a difference between the neoplatonistic philosopher, who sinks into the Absolute and finds the supernatural reality by his feeling of unity with God, and the modern member of a Society for Psychical Research, who discovers the supernatural world by his mathematical calculations on the probable error in telepathic answers about playing-cards! What a difference between the mediæval monk, who becomes convinced of the mystical sphere because the Virgin appears to him in the clouds, and the modern scholar, who is converted because a pathological woman is able to chat about his personal secrets at the rate of twenty francs a sitting! Yet psychology recognizes the common features and understands the mental laws which make mysticism a never-failing element of the social consciousness; the wilder its eccentricities, the more interesting the psychological material.

But the claims of mysticism suggest to the psychologist another attitude less peaceable than that of the observer, the attitude of a rival. If mystics believed only that heavy chairs sometimes fly through the air, that invisible bells ring, and that objects disappear into the fourth dimension, they would have to fight it out with the physicists, but psychology would not interfere. If, inspired by occult advisers, they proposed a new metaphysical theory of the ultimate substratum of the physical universe, the philosophers might stand up as indignant competitors, but the psychologists, again, would have nothing to do with it. The physicians may dispute with the mystics whether the waters of Lourdes are helpful, whether the comets are causes of pestilence, and whether men die on account of being thirteenth at table. There is, perhaps, not a single science, from geometry to theology, which has not its private conflicts with the mystical doctrines; but psychology has no reason to enter the quarrel so long as the mystic does not undertake to answer psychological questions. In this field, however, mysticism has never shown too much modesty. It has at all times, by preference, rioted in the proclamation of mental facts which did not fit into the descriptions and explanations of a sober empirical psychology. If mysticism is right with its old claims, psychology, even with its newest discoveries, is wrong; and thus arises the question, What has the psychologist to say of the claims of mysticism concerning mental processes and the laws of mental action?

These claims have been different at different periods and in different nations, and are still so divergent that no scientist can contend more sharply with the mystical creeds than they contend with one another in the different sets to-day. The telepathists annihilate the theosophists, and the spiritualists belittle the telepathists; and when the Christian scientists and metaphysical healers on the one side, the mind curers and faith curers on the other side, have spoken of each other, there remain few abusive words at the disposal of us outsiders. The average mystic of to-day is a man of high logical ambitions. He looks with contempt on the gypsy who reads your character from the grounds in a coffee-cup, and smiles over the astrological belief that the position of the stars in the hour of your birth has decided your success in love. The medical remedies which have to be cooked at midnight at the churchyard gate are in discredit; and as we live in an enlightened age, it even appears doubtful whether the witches of early time were really under Satanic influences, as their witchcraft can now be "explained" by the telepathic action of mediums, by malicious spirits and materializations. The requirements of mysticism thus shrink to the following main demands. First, the human mind must sometimes be able to perceive in an incomprehensible way the ideas and thoughts of

others. By gradual approaches, this telepathic
talent seems also connected with the power to
have knowledge of distant physical occurrences ;
and if our concessions have reached this point,
we ought not to strain at the little addendum,
the vision of the future. In all cases of this
kind the exceptional talents of the soul are re-
ceptive and passive. A second group of mystical powers may be formed by the corresponding
active influences. In an inconceivable way, it
is assumed, the human mind can control the
thoughts and actions of others ; and here, again,
small steps lead soon to greater and greater mysteries. The mental influence may reach not
only the soul, but also the body of the other
person, and may restore his disturbed health ;
even a child may produce such metaphysical
healing of consumption and heart trouble, can-
cer and broken legs. The mind which by " love "
brings together the fragments of a neighbor's
broken bones ought surely to have no serious
difficulties with the movements of inorganic
bodies : at the bidding of such a mind, tables
fly to the ceiling, and a little stick in the hands
of a weak woman cannot be moved by the
strongest man. A third group refers to the
functions of a deeper self, which is usually hidden under our regular personality. In the most
different trance states, in crystal vision and automatic writing, this mysterious self appears, and

remembers all that we have forgotten, knows many things which we never knew, writes and acts without our control, and shows connections which go far beyond our powers, and mostly even beyond our tastes. Nearly related to these facts is a fourth circle of mystical doctrines, which deal with the psychical deeds of the human spirit after the earthly death. According to these doctrines, the spirits are ready to enter into communication with living men by the help of mediums, with or without materialization, by noises or by table tilting, by slate drawing, and recently even by typewriting. This creed becomes, of course, the starting-point for many denominational divergences.

II

The most natural question is, How far can the regular empirical psychology acknowledge the claimed phenomena? Where is the exact limit which the scientific psychologist is unwilling to pass? He does not discredit perception of voices from far distances if a telephone is included, and he does not doubt that one person may have influence over another in a hundred ways. We must carefully consider where the mystery begins. The attitude of common sense, however, must not be allowed to dictate this line of demarcation; otherwise the psychologist would be bound to denounce all facts which are rare and surprising to the naïve consciousness, or incapable of explanation to the dilettante.   Let us remember that it counts for little whether a fact occurs once a day or once in a century, and that many facts of physiological and pathological psychology must appear to the naïve mind much more surprising and alarming than do the pretensions of the spiritualist.   It seems much simpler and more natural to grant that a little word or figure may wander by mere thought transference from one's mind into the mind of a bystander, than to believe in the startling features of the more complicated cases of hypnotism and somnambulism, hysteria and insanity, all of which find legitimate place in the system of modern psychology.

If we begin with the first two groups of the claims of mystics, — the passive reception of outer psychical and physical events, and the active influence upon other souls and organisms, — we can easily state the general principle which here controls the psychological attitude, though it may often be far from easy to follow up the principle in specific cases.   The psychologist insists that every perception of occurrences outside of one's own body and every influence beyond one's own organism must be intermediated by an uninterrupted chain of physical processes.   The justice of this apparently arbitrary decision may be examined later; at first we ask only for its precise meaning and its consequences. With regard to perception, the limit is certainly sharply drawn, and yet it may be often difficult to recognize it. We perceive only objects which directly or indirectly stimulate our physical sense organs, and which stimulate them by physical means. The perception of a man's body is therefore the primary process; the perception of his thoughts and feelings is secondary, as they must be somehow physically expressed in order to act as stimuli for the sense organs.

In two directions the case may become abnormal: the transmitter or the receiver may differ from the usual type of communicating persons. The transmitter himself, for instance, may not be conscious that he expresses his ideas, or, better, that his ideas discharge themselves in perceptible physical processes. He may blush without knowing it, and thus betray his inner shame; or he may contract the muscles which turn his body toward the outer point he is thinking of; or his breathing or pulse may change through his excitement over a question; and the receiver may be in a situation to become aware of these unintended signals of inner states. Here belongs the well-known stage piece of muscle reading, which is often carelessly confused with real telepathy. It certainly is one of the easily explicable forms of psychophysical communication. Here belong as well all the slight hints by which nervous persons make it possible again and again for confessed impostors to play the rôles of successful mind readers. The pseudo-mediums need only to seek for information in desultory chatting, which, under the high tension of expectancy, suffices to bring about all kinds of unintended expressions which show the clever juggler the way.

The receiver of the physical impressions, also, may differ from the average. We think primarily of the possibility that the receiving instruments — that is, the sense organs or the sensory brain parts and nerve paths — may have become abnormally sensitive, by training or by pathological variations. Through the touch sensation of his face the blind man perceives distant obstacles in his way, to which our untrained central sense apparatus is unresponsive; but that does not conflict with the propositions of psychology, and is not mystical. We know that the threshold for just perceptible sensations is often surprisingly lowered for hypnotic and hysterical subjects, who can thus perceive faint impressions and signals which must escape the normal consciousness. Even if a man were so gifted as to discriminate smells like a dog, or to see the ultra-violet rays, or to perceive solids by the Roentgen rays, or if he had a sense organ for electric currents more sensitive than the finest galvanometer, the psychologist would have no reason for skepticism so long as the physical nature of the transmission from the outer object to the brain is admitted. Other variations in the receiver may be determined by his state of attention. An outer stimulus may reach his brain by the door of his senses without producing an apperceived idea at the moment, but not without influence on his later feelings and actions; a molecular alteration of the brain disposition may last and work as after effect of the stimulation without having attracted the attention at all. This occurrence, also, which in narrow limits is familiar and usual enough, may be pathologically exaggerated, and may then, as for instance in hysterical cases, produce surprising results, if the subject shows undoubted knowledge of facts which he could never have acquired consciously; but this, likewise, nowhere transcends the psychological probabilities.

Still more complicated, perhaps, are the variations in the active power of the mind, within the limits which psychologists willingly acknowledge, or at least ought to acknowledge. Our thoughts and volitions certainly have influence on other minds; we should not speak a word nor write a line if we did not believe that. But again we consider the psychical effects which we produce in others as intermediated by physical processes. We stimulate the optic and acoustic and tactual nerves of others with the purpose of reaching their central nervous system, and of producing there the ideas with which we started. These ideas must then work for themselves; they stir up their associations and awaken their inhibitions, but the outsider cannot add anything further. He can only communicate the ideas, and let them work in the receiver from a psychological point of view; that is all the influence we have on our fellow men.

III

There is one complication of this trivial process of communication which seems to touch the borderland of mysticism, — hypnotic suggestion. The hypnotized subject must do whatever the hypnotizer suggests to him. Here the will of one mind seems to have an incomprehensible influence over the other, and as if it were only a short way from the hypnotic rapport to the influences of mystical character; that is, of a kind which excludes the possibility of physical intermediation. The resemblance is deceptive, however; even the most complicated case of hypnotic influence is based only on elementary actions which occur every moment in our normal mental life. If we want some one to do a thing, we communicate our wish to him, trusting that the idea proposed will discharge itself in the desired motor action. That corresponds fully to our general knowledge that every sensory mental state is at the same time the starting-point of motor impulses. If we say to our neighbor, " Please pass me the cream," we take for granted that the communicated idea will discharge itself in the little action. But if we say, "Please jump out of the window," the result will not be the same. The communicated idea by itself alone would have the effect of producing the action demanded, but it awakens by the regular associative mechanism a set of ideas on the folly of the demand and the danger of the undertaking, and all these associations are starting-points for antagonistic impulses which are finally reinforced by the whole personality : the proposed action is thus inhibited, and the man does not jump. He would jump if the antagonistic idea could be kept down ; and in this case the foolish action would be just as necessarily determined by the conditions and just as natural as the reasonable one. But we all know that this power of ideas to overcome antagonistic associations is quite a normal thing, active in the most varying measure everywhere in our normal mental life.

We call an idea which thus checks the antagonistic one a suggestion, and we may be sure that no education or art, no politics or church life, would be possible without such suggestions. The idea may become a suggestion by the way in which it is presented, but it may also acquire this character by the disposition of the receiver. We know there are stubborn men who contradict every proposition, and there are others who are open to every new idea without inner resistance, and ready to believe everything they hear, or even everything they see in print. They are thus more at the mercy of suggestions; we say they show greater suggestibility. On the other hand, every man's suggestibility is variable; it is increased by fear and other emotions, by alcohol and other nervines, and under special conditions it may reach a pathological intensity. This abnormal degree of suggestibility, in which the antagonistic associations of the suggested ideas are more or less completely inhibited, is the mental state we call hypnotism. If this state of increased suggestibility is reached, the outer action which fulfills the proposed suggestion becomes, through the regular psychophysical mechanism, unavoidable. The final results, to be sure, may appear surprisingly different from the normal actions of the personality, but even the most absurd hypnotic action is based on these simple psychological principles. As, theoretically, everybody can hypnotize everybody, it is obvious that no special mystical power need be invoked at this point; and even if we induce the hypnotized subject to do a criminal action, it is no mysterious power with which we overcome his honesty, but a combination of processes

which are neither clearer nor more obscure than
normal attention and association. There is not
the slightest reason to consider hypnotism, with
all its ramifications, as in any degree mystical
because of its weird and alarming results. We
may not understand every detail as yet, but
nothing need suggest any doubt that other principles are involved than those in daily mental
activity. Hypnotism is free from responsibility
for mystical theories. Mysticism, on the other
hand, cannot hope to pass through the entrance
door of science on account of its superficial similarity to some hypnotic cases.

Practically, the two may be mixed till they
are indistinguishable. In spiritualistic séances
the plain hypnotic phenomena are not seldom
used to smooth the way for the telepathic mysticism, as criticism of the latter will be less sharp
if the first part of the performance is undoubtedly reliable. If there is no physical intermediation between the transmitter and the receiver,
thought transference remains mystical, and whether the receiver is hypnotized or not has nothing
to do with the case. No change is involved
by the belief of the subject, no matter how sincere, that he is under such mystical influence
from far distances. Only a short time ago I
had such a case under my observation. There
came to me, late at night, a stranger, in wildest
despair, resolved to commit suicide that night if

I could not help him.   He had been a physician, but had given up his practice because his
brother, on the other side of the ocean, hated
him and had him under his telepathic influence,
troubling him from over the sea with voices
which mocked him and with impulses to foolish
actions. He had not slept nor had he eaten
anything for several days, and the only chance
for life he saw was that a new hypnotic influence might overpower the mystical hypnotic
forces. I soon found the source of his trouble.
In treating himself for a wound he had misused
cocaine in an absurd way, and the hallucination
of voices was the chief symptom of his cocain-
ism.   These products of his poisoned brain
had sometimes reference to his brother in Europe,
and thus the telepathic idea grew in him and
permeated his whole life.   I hypnotized him,
and suggested to him with success to have sleep
and food and a smaller dose of cocaine.   Then
I hypnotized him daily for six weeks. After
ten days he gave up cocaine entirely, after three
weeks the voices disappeared, and after that the
other symptoms faded away. It was not, however,
until the end that the telepathic theory was ex-
ploded. Even when the voices had gone, he
felt for a while that his movements were controlled from over the ocean; and after six
weeks, when I had made him quite well again,
he laughed over his telepathic absurdities, but

assured me that if these sensations came again he should be unable, even in full health, to resist the mystical interpretation, so vividly had he felt the distant influences.

IV

This case may bring us to another main group of personal influences, the therapeutical ones. The man of common sense is more suspicious of fraud in this field than anywhere else, and yet the psychologist must here concede as possible a greater part of the claimed facts than in the other domains of mysticism. He will reject a good deal, it is true, and in acknowledging the rest of the facts he will not think of committing himself to the theories; yet he must feel sorry that truth demands from him the acknowledgment of anything, not because he thinks himself bound to advertise the regular practicing physician, but because he knows how these facts carry with them a flock of contagious confusing ideas. Seen from the standpoint of the psychologist, the line between the possible and the mysterious healing influences of personality is fairly though not absolutely sharp. We have seen that every normal psychophysical state has the tendency to go over into peripheral bodily processes. We have so far noticed only the processes in the voluntary muscles, the so-called actions, and we have found that there is no special power involved and that no mystery need be invoked, but that every idea discharges itself in an action provided the antagonistic ideas are checked. But the motor nerves and muscular apparatus represent only a part of the central and centrifugal system which can be stimulated by sensory processes. The researches of physiology have fully proved that our involuntary muscles and our blood-vessels, our glands and our internal organs, are under the influence of our central system. Our whole body in every instant resounds in every part to the variations of our brain activity, and the normal functioning of our organism depends in a large degree on the right work of these central stimulations. Are they absent or inhibited, something must go wrong; and if the central stimulus can be enforced, if the antagonistic inhibition can be checked, the right tension and the normal functioning must return as necessarily and as naturally as the suggested action must occur when the contradicting ideas are removed. We have seen that hypnotism is nothing but a psychophysical state of increased suggestibility; that is, a state in which the suggested ideas find less resistance than in normal life. If the hypnotized patient receives suggestions which refer to those physiological functions which are dependent upon the central nervous system, the change and the readjustment of the organic functions by the removal of false inhibitions and by the reinforcement of useful central stimulations are certainly no more obscure than the action of antipyrine and phenacetine. Even that which may be still obscure in the action of the suggestions can be only a matter of details, not of principles.

There are two methods of suggestion open: a more active and talkative way, which turns the subject's attention to the desired point by direct suggestions, and a more passive and silent way, which attempts a general quieting of the mind, in which a new balance of impulses may be inaugurated, and the desire for normal functions may work itself up to increased influence. Every good physician makes use of these two means to increase the effectiveness of his remedies. At the right time, they are almost a substitute for all other aid, and in the mystical therapy of all periods through four thousand years they have developed a high technique. To-day, the passive method of indirect suggestion is the vehicle of the Christian scientists and metaphysical healers; the active way of more direct suggestion belongs to the mind curers and mental healers.

Much of the success of both methods depends, of course, upon the ability of the transmitter to make the suggestions effective. His personal appearance and way of talking, his voice and temperament, must be persuasive, and his reputation and authority must reinforce the expectancy which prepares the inhibitions. Teachers and lawyers and ministers strengthen their influence by these silent servants of a dominant mind. Many of these personal qualities can be replaced, to be sure, by merely mechanical tricks which can be imitated and taught. Our mystical schools bring this technique to external virtuosity. But still more important are the antecedent conditions in the mind of the patient. Whoever has seen the patients in the clinic of a famous hypnotist (half hypnotized as soon as they pass the door of the hospital) knows how the fascination of the attention by belief — by any belief — works favorably for the increase of suggestibility; so that the smallest additional intruder, perhaps the sensation of half-darkened light, of soft touch, of muscle strain in the eyes, is sufficient to bring about the new equilibrium of psychophysical impulses. The most vulgar and trivial belief will answer; the most absurd superstition can bring success, as everything depends upon the intensity of the subject's submission; and the more pitiable the intellectual powers of a creature, the greater may be his chance of a cure by idiotic manipulations. To deny this in the interest of science would be unscientific.

The most deep-seated form of belief is religious faith, and there cannot be the slightest doubt that religious emotion, from the lowest fetichism to the highest protestantism, has always been fertile soil for therapeutical suggestions. What we have called the active method appeals to the subjective faith with direct words; the passive method awakens the same fascination indirectly, lulling to sleep the antagonistic impulses by a feeling that the mind of the transmitter has reached by prayer and love a supernatural unity with the mind of the patient. We must not forget that it is not the solemn value of the religious revelation, nor the ethical and metaphysical bearing of its objects, which brings success, but solely the depth of the emotion. To murmur the Greek alphabet with the touching intonation and gesture of supplication is just as strengthening for the health as the sublimest prayer; and for the man who believes in the metaphysical cure, it may be quite unimportant whether the love curer at his bedside thinks of the psychical Absolute or of the spring hat she will buy with the fee for her metaphysical healing. From the psychological point of view, the direct method of healing by faith and the indirect method of healing by love are thus almost identical; both are confined to the narrow limits within which the nervous system influences the pathological processes; but in these limits both have some chances of a transitory success, and both are liable to the same illusions on the part of sincere healers and to the same humbug on the part of impostors.

V

Our review has sought to examine the two large groups of facts which refer to the influence of mind on mind, and to separate in both, in those of active influence and in those of passive reception, the psychological possibilities from those claims which the psychologist at first rejects. There are two groups more which we must sift, — the facts which lead to the theory of double consciousness, and the spiritualistic facts which refer to the communication of the living with the souls of the dead. In the former group there is little fault to be found with the facts ; only the theory is misleading. In the latter group, on the other hand, it may be difficult to decide whether the claims for the facts or the attempts at theories are the more objectionable. The phenomena which suggest that a deeper personality lies hidden under the experiences of our surface personality are to-day generally familiar and scientifically well studied. Typical of these phenomena are the interesting facts of automatic writing, apart from the attempts to give them a spiritualistic interpretation. Our hands may be brought to write truths of which we are not conscious, and to answer questions which we do not perceive ; and

these writings which we do not control may
clearly belong to a special personality, with its
own memory and its own wit and temper. Many
similar facts which do not necessarily point in
the same direction presuppose hysterical disturbances. It is true that the idea of a separated
subject of consciousness offers itself to a superficial view as the simplest hypothesis, and the
acceptance of this hypothesis gives a foothold
for the most complicated mystical theories. But
there are two groups of facts which we must
keep in mind. First, we know that all our complicated useful actions which are acquired under
the control of the intellectual attention, as
walking and eating, speaking and reading and
writing, become slowly automatic, yet nobody
thinks of putting them under the care of a
deeper personality; we make the right movement in speaking without consciously intending
the special tongue and lip movements, because
the lower nerve centres steadily unburden the
higher ones, and more and more easily transform the stimulus into the useful motor discharge. Even in the most complicated cases,
therefore, the unconscious production of apparently chosen and adapted actions is no proof
whatever that the whole process was not a merely
physiological one. Secondly, a manifoldness of
psychological personalities is in no way identical
with a plurality of subjects of consciousness.

Every one of us finds in his consciousness a
bundle of social personalities. We are different
men in the office and in the family circle, in the
political meeting and in the theatre; one does
not care for the others, and may even ignore
them; each has his own memory connection and
his own impulses. But they do not represent
different subjects of consciousness, different
groups of objects alternating in the same subject. Of course these various empirical personalities have always some elements in common,
by which we can easily bridge over from one to
the other, and remember our office anger in
front of the stage of the theatre. No change
in principle occurs when, by an abnormal brain
process, these paths of association and connection are blocked, and one personality remains
without relations with the other. In such a case
several personalities alternate, each consisting of
a set of associations and impulses without remem-
brance of the others. The student of hypnotism
and hysteria is familiar with such phenomena.
These personalities alternate in consciousness in
the same way that groups of ideas succeed one
another; but the subject which is the bearer of
all these personalities remains always the same,
and the hypothesis that this subject itself
changes when the content of the social personality changes is thus without support in the
psychological interpretations of the normal idea

of personality. The real source of these theories as to a deeper self and a double consciousness lies, indeed, not in the psychological facts,
but in motives of a very different character.
We shall turn presently to these more hidden
impulses, as they will show us the real springs
of mysticism; but we must first glance at our
fourth and last group of claims, — the wonders
of spiritualism.

So long as we consider spiritualism only from
the point of view of its agreement with the system of scientific psychology, the discussion may
be extremely short, for one sweeping word is
sufficient. There are no subtle discriminations
necessary, as in the other fields: the psychologist rejects everything without exception. We
have here not the slightest relation to philosophical spiritualism, either to that of the Berke-
leian type or to that of Fichte. We are not on
the height of philosophical thinking, but on the
low ground of observation and explanation of
empirical facts. The question is not whether
the substance of the real world is spiritual; it is
only whether departed spirits enter into communication with living men by mediums and
by incarnation. The scientist does not admit a
compromise: with regard to this he flatly denies
the possibility. Of course he does not say that
all the claims are founded on fraud. He does
not deny that sincere persons have frequently

believed, through hallucinations, and still oftener
through illusions, that they saw the apparitions
of departed friends and heard their voices. The
psychologist has no dearth of explanations for
this product of the psychophysical mechanism.
In the same way, he need not doubt that many
of the mediums really believe themselves to be
under the control of departed souls; for this
also exactly fits many well-known facts of nervous disturbance. But the facts as they are
claimed do not exist, and never will exist, and
no debate makes the situation better.

VI

Our short survey of the wide domain of mysticism is finished. We have seen what part of
its claims can be acknowledged by psychology,
and what must be rejected. We have seen that
many of those occurrences which appear mysterious and uncanny to the naïve mind are easily
understood from a scientific point of view, and
are often separated by an impassable chasm from
happenings which on the surface look quite
similar. We have seen especially that hypnotism
and hysteria, muscle reading and hyperæsthesia,
alternation of personality and the therapeutic influence of psychophysical inhibitions, hallucinations and illusions, and other mental states which
psychology understands just as well as it does
the normal associations and feelings, explain

many of the observed events, and bring them
from the domain of mysticism into the sphere of
causally necessary processes. And yet all this
is only a preamble for our real discussion. We
have given decisions, but not arguments; we
have shown that psychology is able to explain
many of the facts, but we have not shown as
yet why we have the right to reject other so-
called facts and to deny their possibility; and
everything must at last depend upon this right
alone.

The modern mystic, if he is ready to follow
us thus far, would not find the slightest argument against his position in any of our preceding points. He would say: "I accept your
psychophysical explanations for the facts which
you acknowledge; with regard to the others, I
see only that you are unable to understand them,
but that gives you no right to deny them.
There are many facts which are still puzzles for
science. History must make us modest, showing that again and again the truth was at first
ridiculed and the deeper insight derided. These
very phenomena of hypnotism and automatism
and hysteria were denied in their reality only a
few generations ago. Science must give everything fair play, and a refusal even to examine
the facts is unworthy of real science. It is nar-
rowness and stubbornness to reject a fact because it does not fit into the scientific system of

to-day, instead of striving toward the better system of to-morrow, which will have room for all
the phenomena ; and this the more if these facts
are of vast importance, involving the immortality and the absolute unity of all minds, the
spiritual harmony of the universe, and the very
deepest powers of man."

This is the old text, indeed, preached from so
often, and sometimes in so brilliant and fascina-
ting a style that even the best men have lowered
the sword. Yet it is wrong and dangerous from
beginning to end, and has endlessly more harm
in it than a superficial view reveals, as it is in
its last consequences not only the death of real
science, but worse, — the death of real idealism.

First a word about the so-called facts. Our
newspapers, magazines, and books are full to
overflowing of the reports of happenings which
no science can explain, and which may over-
whelm the uncritical mind by their sheer bulk.
But whoever stops to think for a moment how
the psychological conditions favor and almost
enforce the weedlike growth of mysterious stories will at least agree that a live criticism must
sift the tales, even if they are backed by the authority of a most trustworthy sailor or a most
excellent servant girl. If the glaring light of
criticism is thrown on this twilight literature, the
effect is often surprising. Some of the " facts "
prove to be simply untrue, having grown up

through gossip and desire for excitement, through
fear and curiosity, through misunderstandings
and imagination. Another set of the "facts"
turns out to be true, but not mysterious; being
merely a checkered field of abnormal mental
phenomena, such as hypnotism, somnambulism,
hysteria, insanity, hyperæsthesia, automatic action, and so forth. Another large group is based
on conscious or unconscious fraud, from the
mildest form down through a long scale to the
boldest spiritualistic forgery. If we take away
these three large groups, there is a remainder
which may deserve discussion as to its interpretation. Here belong the chance occurrences
which appear alarmingly surprising if taken in
isolation, but quite natural if considered as members of a long series, giving account of all the
cases in which the surprising coincidences did
not occur. The recent statistics of apparitions
and hallucinations show clearly the difficulty of
finding always the right basis for such calculation of mathematical probabilities. Here belong,
further, the illusions of memory, by which present experiments are projected into the past, or
past experiences are transformed by present sensations; the surprising coincidences illustrated
by recent experiments, which are produced by
the concordance of associations and other simi-
larities of mental dispositions; and the illusions
of perception which allow us to hear and see

whatever we expect or whatever is suggested to us.

If we are ready to make full use of every means of possible explanation, there remains hardly an instance where it is impossible to tear aside the veil of mystery, and to explain psychologically either the occurrences of the facts themselves, or the development of the erroneous report about them. Even when long series of careful experiments on thought transference and similar problems were made, the cautious papers discreetly reported in most cases, not that a proof was furnished, but only that the evidence seemed to point in a certain direction. And even the most ardent believer in telepathy, Mr. Podmore, concedes that "each particular case is susceptible of more or less adequate explanation by some well-known cause." Mr. Podmore considers it absurd to accumulate the strained and complicated explanations which thus become necessary, instead of accepting the simple wholesale interpretation that telepathy took place. But with the same right we might say that in an endless number of instances the lowest animals and plants rise from inorganic substances ; each case taken separately could be explained by biologists from procreation, but since such explanation would involve an accumulation of complicated theories about the conditions of life for the lowest animals, it would be much simpler to believe in *generatio equivoca*.

Our presupposition was that a large proportion of the claims are false. Even the cham-
pions of mysticism are to-day ready to admit that
the temptations and chances for deception are
discouragingly numerous. Not only is there an
abundance of money-making schemes which fit
well the natural credulity and suggestibility of
the public at large. Some lie and cheat merely
for art's sake, getting pleasure from the fact that
their fiction becomes real through the belief that
it awakes, and some do the same merely in boy-
ish trickery. Some elaborate their inventions to
make themselves interesting, and some feast in
the power they thus gain over men. Some
begin by consciously embellishing the slender
facts, and end with a sincere belief in their own
superstructure ; and others, through hysterical
excitement, are unaware of their own cheating.
Add to these causes the incorrectness with which
most men observe and report on matters in
which their feelings are interested, and the miserable lack of the feeling of responsibility with
which average men and average papers put forth
their wild tales. Consider how again and again
the honored leaders of mystical movements have
been unmasked as cheap impostors and their
admired wonders recognized as vulgar tricks,
how telepathic performances have been reduced
to a simple signaling by breathing or noises,
and how seldom disbelievers have interrupted a

materialization séance without putting their hands on a provision of beards and draperies. Think of all this, and the supposed facts dwindle more and more.

At this point of the discussion the friends of mysticism like to go over to a more personal attack. They say, "How do you dare to presuppose credulity and suggestibility in the observer, and intended or unintended tricks and dishonesty in the performer, when you have never taken part in such experiments, and when some brilliant scholars have examined them and found no fraud?" To such personal reproach I answer with personal facts. It is true I have never taken part in a telepathic experiment or in a spiritualistic séance. It is not a nervous dislike of abnormalities which has kept me away, as I have devoted much time to the study of hypnotism and insanity. The experiences of some of my friends, however, made me cautious from the beginning; they had spent much energy and time and money on such mysteries, and had come to the conviction that all was humbug. Once, I confess, I wavered in my decision. In Europe I received a telegram from two famous telepathists asking me to come immediately to a small town where they had discovered a medium of extraordinary powers. It required fifteen hours' traveling, and I hesitated; but the report was so inspiring that I finally packed my trunks. Just then came a second message with the laconic words, " All fraud." Since that time I do not take the trouble to pack. I wait quietly for the second message.

Why do I avoid these séances? It is not because I am afraid that they would shake my theoretical views and convince me of mysticism, but because I consider it undignified to visit such performances, as one attends a variety show, for amusement only, without attempting to explain them, and because I know that I should be the last man to see through the scheme and discover the trick. I should certainly have been deceived by Madame Blavatsky, the theosophist, and by Miss Paladino, the medium. I am only a psychologist, not a detective. More than that, by my whole training I am absolutely spoiled for the business of the detective. The names of great scientists, like Zoellner, Richet, Crookes, and many others, do not impose on me in the least; for their daily work in scientific laboratories was a continuous training of an instinctive confidence in the honesty of their coöperators. I do not know another profession in which the suspicion of possible fraud becomes so systematically inhibited as it does in that of the scientist. He ought to be at once dismissed from the jury, and a prestidigitator substituted. Whether I personally take part in such meetings or not is, therefore, without any

consequences; I take it for granted from the
start that wherever there was fraud in the play,
I should have been cheated like my brethren.
The only thing that the other side can reason-
ably demand from us is that we be fully ac-
quainted with their claims and with the evidence
they furnish in their writings. I confess I have
not had quite a good conscience in this respect;
I had not really studied all the recorded Phan-
tasms of the Living and all the Proceedings of
the Societies for Psychical Research, and I am
afraid I had forgotten to cut the leaves of some of
the occult magazines on my own shelves. Now,
however, my conscience is fully disburdened. I
used — or ought I to say, misused? — my last
summer vacation in working through more than
a hundred volumes of the so-called evidence. I
passed through a whole series of feelings. Indeed, I had at first a feeling of mysterious
excitement from all those uncanny stories, but
that changed into a deep æsthetical and ethical
disgust, which flattened finally into the feeling
that there was about me an endless desert of
absolute stupidity. I, for one, am to-day far
more skeptical than before I was driven to examine the evidence; I have studied the proofs,
and now feel sure of what before I only suspected, — that they do not prove anything; and
if we condemn science on such testimony, we do
worse than those who condemned the witches and

vampires. In short, I believe that the facts, if
they are examined critically, are never incapable
of a scientific explanation; and yet even this is
not the central point of the question. I must
deny that the battle is waged over the facts
which science understands and those which it
does not understand.

VII

No scientist in the world feels uncomfortable
over the confession that there are many — endlessly many — things in the world which we do
not know; no sane man dreams that the last
day of scientific progress has yet come, and that
every problem has been solved. On the contrary, the springs of scientific enthusiasm lie in
the conviction that we stand only at the beginning
of knowledge, and that every day may unveil
new elements of the universe. Even physiological psychology, which seems so conceited in
the face of mysticism, admits how meagre is the
knowledge it has so far gleaned. Almost every
important question of our science is still un-
settled, and yet that has never discouraged us in
our work. The physicist and the astronomer,
the chemist and the botanist, the physiologist
and the psychologist, work steadily, with the
conviction that there are many facts which they
do not know, like the Roentgen rays ten years
ago, and that many facts are not fully under-

stood, like the Roentgen rays at present. If the mystical facts were merely processes which we do not understand to-day, but which we may understand to-morrow, there would not be the slightest occasion for a serious dispute. But the situation is very different. The antithesis is not between the facts we can explain and the facts we cannot explain, and for which we seek an explanation of the same order. No; it is between the facts which are now explicable by causal laws, or may be so in any possible future, and those facts which are acknowledged as in principle outside of the necessary causal connections, and bound together by their values for our personal feelings instead of by mechanical laws. As Professor James puts it excellently: It is the difference between the personal emotional and the impersonal mechanical thinking, between the romantic and the rationalistic views of the world. Here lies the root of the problem, and here centres our whole interest. Indeed, all that is claimed by the mystic as such means, not that the causal connections of the world found so far are still incomplete and must be supplemented by others, but that the blanks in the causal connections allow us glimpses of another world behind, — an uncausal emotional world which shines through the vulgar world of mechanics.

If the astronomer calculated the movement of

a star from the causally working forces, he might
come to the hypothesis that there are centres of
attraction existing which we have not yet discovered : it was thus Leverrier discovered Neptune.
But his boldest theories operate only with quan-
tities of the same order, with substances and
forces which come under the categories of the
mechanical world.   If, on the other hand, he
considered some emotional view, perhaps the
æsthetical one that the star followed this curve
because it is more beautiful, as indeed an older
astronomy did; or the ethical one that this
movement of the star occurred because it served
to make the moral progress of men possible,
while the causal movement would have thrown
the earth into the sun; or the religious one
that the angels chose to pull the star this way
rather than that; or the poetical one that the
star was obliged to move just so in order to
delight the heart on a clear evening by its spar-
kling, — in none of these cases would he be
doubtful whether his hypothesis were good or
bad; he would be sure that it was not an astro-
nomical hypothesis at all.   He would not search
with the telescope to find out whether or not his
theory was confirmed by new facts.   No; he
would see that his thought denied the possibility
of astronomy, and was a silly profanation of
ethics and religion at the same time.

The naturalist knows, if he understands the

philosophical basis of his work, and is not merely a technical craftsman, that natural science means, not a simple cast and copy of the reality, but a special transformation of reality, a conceptual construction of unreal character in the service of special logical purposes. The naturalist does not think that bodies are in reality made from atoms, and that the movements of the stars are really the products of all the elementary impulses into which his calculation disintegrates the causes. He knows that all his elements, the elementary substances and the elementary forces, are merely conceptions worked out for the purpose of representing the world as a causally connected mechanism. The real world is no mechanism, but a world of means and aims, objects of our will and of our personal purposes. But one of these purposes is to conceive the world as a mechanism, and so long as we work in the service of this purpose we presuppose that the world is a mechanism. In the effort to represent the world as a causal one — that is, in our character as naturalists — we know only a causal world, and no other. We may know little about that postulated causal world, but we are sure beforehand that whatever the future may discover about it must belong to the causal system, or it is wrong. We are free to choose the point of view, but when we have chosen it we are bound by its presuppositions. A naturalist who begins to doubt whether the world is everywhere causal misunderstands his own aim and gives up his only end.

These simple facts from the methodology of science repeat themselves exactly, though in a more complicated form, for psychology. Psychology, also, is never a mere copy of the reality, but always a transformation in the service of a special logical purpose. Our real inner life is not a complex of elementary sensations, as psychology may see it: it is a system of attitudes of will, which we do not perceive as contents of consciousness, but which we live through, and objects of will which are our means and ends and values. It becomes a special interest of the logical attitude of the will to transform this real will system in conceptual form into a causal system, too, and, in the service of this end, to put in the place of the teleological reality a mechanical artificial construction. This construction is psychology, and it is thus clear that in the psychological system itself every view which is not causal is contradictory to the presuppositions, and therefore scientifically untrue. Between the mental facts, in so far as they are considered as psychological phenomena, there exists no other possible connection than the causal one, though, to be sure, this causal view has not the slightest meaning for the inner reality, which never consists of psychological phenomena. This is the point which even philosophers so easily overlook: as soon as we speak of psychical objects, of ideas and feelings and volitions, as contents of consciousness, we speak of an artificial transformation to which the categories of real life no longer apply, — a transformation which lies in the direction of causal connection, and which has, therefore, a right to existence only if the right to extend the causal aspect of nature to the inner life is acknowledged. The personal, the emotional, the romantic, in short the will-view, controls our real life, but from that standpoint mental life is never a psychical fact.

It is one of the greatest dangers of our time that the naturalistic point of view, which decomposes the world into elements for the purpose of causal connection, interferes with the volitional point of view of the real life, which can deal only with values, and not with elements. I have sought again and again to point out this unfortunate situation, and to show that history and practical life, education and art, morality and religion, have nothing to do with these psychological constructions, and that the categories of psychology must not intrude into their teleological realms. But that does not blind me to the fact that exactly the opposite transgression of boundaries is going on all the time, too. If the world of values is intruded into the causal world, if the categories which belong to reality are forced on the system of transformation which was framed in the service of causality, we get a cheap mixture which satisfies neither the one aim nor the other. Just this is the effort of mysticism. It is the personal, emotional view applied, not to the world of reality, where it fits, but to the physical and psychical worlds, both of which are constructed by the human logical will for the purpose of an impersonal, unemotional causal system. But to mix values with laws destroys not only the causal links, but also the values. The ideals of ethics and religion, instead of growing in the world of volitional relations, are now projected into the atomistic structure, and thus become dependent upon its nature. Intended to fill there the blanks in the causal system, they find their right of existence only where ignorance of nature leaves such blanks, and must tremble at every step of progress science makes. It is bad enough when the psychological categories are wrongly pushed into ethics by the over-extension of psychology, but it is still more absurd when ethics leaves its home in the real world and creeps over to the field of psychology, satisfied with the few places to which science has not yet acquired a clear title. Our ethics and religion may thus be shaken to-morrow by any new result of laboratory research, and must be supported to-day by

the telepathic performances of hysteric women.
Our belief in immortality must rest on the gossip which departed spirits utter in dark rooms
through the mouths of hypnotized business mediums, and our deepest personality comes to light
when we scribble disconnected phrases in automatic writing. Is life then really still worth
living ?

VIII

We must here throw more light on some
details which may be difficult to understand.
We have said that the claims of mysticism impose the emotional teleological categories upon
the psychological facts ; that is, upon constructions which are formed for the purpose of the
mechanical categories only. It may not be at
once evident how this is true for special propositions of a mystical nature. Of course we cannot develop here the presuppositions of psychology ; a few words to show the nature of the
problems must be sufficient. Psychology tries
to consider the mental life as a system of perceivable objects which are necessarily determined ;
every transformation which is serviceable for this
purpose is psychologically true. If the mental
facts are thought as determining one another,
we must presuppose that they have characteristics to which this effective influence attaches.
These characteristics are called their elements,

and therefore, for psychologists, the mental life
consists of elements.   The psychical material is
different from the physical by the presupposition
that it exists for one subject only.   It is therefore not communicable ; since incommunicable,
it is not determinable by communicable units,
and hence is not measurable, — not quantitative,
but only qualitative.   Consequently, it is incapable of entering into a mathematical equation, and
is unfit to play the rôle of determinable causes
and effects.   Before psychical elements can be
transformed into a system of causes and effects
a further transformation must be made ; they
must be thought as amalgamated with physical
processes which exist for many, and which are
measurable, and therefore capable of forming a
necessary causal system.   The psychical facts
are thus thought of as accompaniments of physical processes, and in their appearance and disap-
pearance fully determined by the physical events.
There is no materialistic harm in this doctrine,
as it aims at no reference to reality, but is merely
a construction for a special purpose ; within its
sphere, however, there cannot be any exception.
If the psychical facts are thought of as accompaniments of the physical processes, they must be
projected into the physical world, and must
accept its forms of existence, space and time.
The real inner life in its teleological reality is
spaceless and timeless, — it knows space and

time only as forms of its objects; the psychological phenomena themselves enter into space and time as soon as they are connected with the physical phenomena. They are now psychophysical elements which can determine one another only by the causal relations of the physical substratum. The working hypothesis of modern psychology — that every mental state is a complex of psychical elements, of which each is the accompaniment of a physical process in time and space, and influences others or is influenced by others merely through the medium of physical processes — is then not an arbitrary theory. It is the necessary outcome of the presuppositions which the human will has freely chosen for its logical purposes, and to which it is bound by its own decision.

From this point a full light of explanation falls upon all our earlier decisions. We rejected every claimed fact in which the psychological facts were without a physical substratum, as in the case of departed spirits and those in which psychical facts influenced one another without physical intermediation, as in telepathy. If mental life is taken in its reality, it must not be considered as composed of elements, ideas, and feelings, but must be taken as a whole; then it is not in bodily personalities, not in space and not in time, — in short, is not a psychological fact at all. But if we take it as psychological fact in human bodies and in time, it must be thought of in accordance with the psychological presuppositions, as bound to the physical events, communicated by their intermediation and disappearing at their destruction. Where these conditions are in part wanting, psychology declines to accept the propositions as truths, and demands a further transformation of the facts till the demands of psychology are satisfied. Mysticism, however, prefers an easier way. Wherever the conditions of psychological truth are absent, and, owing to the lack of physical substrata or of physical mediation, the psychical facts are disconnected or unexplained in their existence, there mysticism imports the teleological links of the prepsychological real world, and gives the illusion that the psychical facts have been thus explained and connected.

Perhaps most instructive in this respect are those claims of mysticism which refer to the healing influences of men, because here it appears most clearly that it is not the facts, but only the points of view, which constitute the mysticism. The facts from which these claims arise the psychologist does not deny at all; as we have seen, he takes them for granted. But he explains them by suggestion and other familiar laws of mental action, and thus links the psychical phenomena by an uninterrupted chain of physical processes. The mystic, on the other hand, brings the same facts under the categories which belong to the world of values: prayer has now a healing influence, not because it is perceived by the senses of the patient, and works through association some inhibitory changes in his brain, but because prayer is ethically and religiously valuable. Not its physiological accompaniments which produce psychophysical effects, but its goodness and piety secure success, and, conversely, the illness which is cured by the prayer must be a symptom of moral and religious obliquity. The causal conception of a disturbance of physiological functions is thus transmuted into the ethical conception of sin. Exactly the same psychophysical facts, the prayer of the transmitter and the feeling of improvement in the receiver, are in this case, then, connected by the mystic and the scientist in different ways, without any need on either side of a further transformation of the facts. For the one, it is the causal process that a suggestion psychophysically overpower nervous inhibition ; for the other, it is the victory of sainthood over sin, by its religious values. If the scientist maintains that only the first is an explanatory connection, the second not, does he mean by this that goodness has no power over evil ? Certainly not ; he means something very different. Goodness and evil, he thinks, are relations and attitudes of will, which have their

reality in being willed and lived through. They
are not psychophysical facts, to be perceived as
taking time, and going on in space in a special
brain and nervous system. They belong to the
world of willing subjects, not to the world of
atomistic objects; they are primary, while suggestions and inhibitions and all the other psychophysical objects are unreal derived constructions.
If prayer and sin are taken in their reality as we
live through them, then of course their meaning
and their value alone are in question, and it
would be absurd to apply to them the relations
of causal connection. As realities, they are not
brain processes; as such, they do not come in
question as processes in time and space; as such,
they are not transmuted into mere objects. If
we take them in their reality as will-attitudes,
they have no relation to causality. If we take
them as psychological processes which go on in
time in physical personalities, then we have
transformed them in the service of causality, and
have pledged ourselves to the causal system.
An ethical connection of psychophysical facts is
a direct inner contradiction; it means applying
the categories of will to objects which we have
taken away from the will for the single purpose
of putting them into a system of will-less categories. We might just as well demand that the
figures of a painting should talk and move
about.

IX

Another case in which scientists and mystics agree in regard to the facts is that of double personality. The difference here, also, is only one of interpretation. We have seen that the psychologist understands this class of facts as various degrees of disaggregation of psychophysical elements, whereas the mystic introduces the ethical categories of different responsibility and dignity. It is otherwise with the telepathic or spiritualistic claims : here there is no agreement about the facts, and yet the principle is the same as in the other cases. The mystic applies the emotional personal links in this case, also, not to the reality, but to psychological facts in a stage of transformation which the psychologist does not accept because they do not allow causal connection. The psychologist calls the claimed facts untrue, because the transformation of reality is psychologically or physically true only when it has reached that form in which it fits into the causal system. It is the aim of science to find the true facts, — that is, to transform reality till the ends of causal ordering are attained ; and if they are not attained, the objects have not become a part of the existing psychological or physical world. An infinite number of facts appear to us in disconnected form, but we ignore them ; they remain only propositions ;

they have not existence, because they do not fulfill the conditions upon which, according to the decision of the will which produces science, psychical or physical existence depends. That a fact is true in the world of psychical facts means that it is selected as fit for a special logical purpose; and if the telepathic facts, for instance, are not suited to that purpose, they are not true according to the only consistent standard of truth. They must become somehow otherwise; that is, they must be transformed until they can be accepted as existing. The history of science constantly demonstrates this necessity. It is absurd for the mystics to claim the backing of history because it shows that many things are acknowledged as true to-day which were not believed in earlier times. The teaching of history, on the contrary, annihilates almost cruelly every claim of mysticism, as, far from a later approval of mystical wisdom, history has in every case remoulded the facts till they have become causal ones. If the scientists of earlier times disbelieved in phenomena as products of witchcraft, and believe to-day in the same phenomena as products of hypnotic suggestion and hysteria, the mystics are not victorious, but defeated. As long as the ethical category of Satanic influence was applied to the appearances they were not true; as soon as they were brought under the causal categories they were accepted as true, but they were then no longer mystical,—it was not witchcraft any more.

This process of transformation goes on steadily; millions of propositions which life suggests remain untrue till they are adjusted. Just this would be the fate of the telepathic propositions: they would remain below the threshold of the world of empirical facts, if a mistaken emotional attitude did not awaken the illusion that there exists here a connection capable of satisfying the demand for explanation. The personal importance then links what ought to be linked by impersonal causality. A feeling of depression in the psychophysical organism and the death of a friend a thousand miles distant have for us no causal connection, but an emotional one. The two events have no relation in the sphere of objects; they are connected only in the sphere of will-acts; and the link is not the goodness, as in the case of healing by prayer, but the emotional importance of the death for the friend's feeling attitude. By this will-connection the two phenomena are selected and linked together, and offer themselves as one fact, while without that emotional unity they would remain disconnected, and therefore in this combination they would not be accepted in the sphere of empirical facts.

Does the scientist maintain, in his opposition to telepathy, that in reality mental communication between subjects is possible only by physical intermediation? Decidedly not. If I talk with others whom I wish to convince, there is no physical process in question; mind reaches mind, thought reaches thought; but in this aspect thoughts are not psychophysical phenomena in space and time, but attitudes and propositions in the sphere of the will. If we take our mental life in its felt reality, then the emotional conviction that no physical wall intervenes between mind and mind is the only correct one; it would be even meaningless to look for physical connection. But if we transform the reality into psychological objects in time and in bodies, then we are bound by the aim of the transformation, and we can acknowledge their connection as true only if it is a mechanical one.

Finally, the ethical demand for immortality, when applied to the artificial construction of psychology instead of to the real life, brings out the most repulsive claim of mysticism, — spiritualism. The ethical belief in immortality means that we as subjects of will are immortal; that is, that we are not reached by death. For the philosophical mind which sees the difference between reality and psychological transformation, immortality is certain; for him, the denial of immortality would be even quite meaningless. Death is a biological phenomenon in the world of objects in time; how then can death reach a reality which is not an object, but an attitude, and therefore neither in time nor in space? Our real inner subjective life has its felt validity, not in time, but beyond time; it is eternal. We have seen why the purpose of psychology demands that this non-local and non-temporal subjectivity shall be transformed into a psychical object, and as such projected into the space- and time - filling organism. By that demand the mental life itself becomes a process in time; and if the ethical demand for immortality is now transplanted into this circle of constructed phenomena, there must result a clash between psychology and human emotion. Conceiving mental life as a process in time was done merely for the purpose of representing it as the accompaniment of physical phenomena, and now to demand that it should go on in time after the destruction of this physical substratum is absurd. In so far as we conceive mental life as an artificial psychological process in time, in so far we think of it only as part of a psychophysical phenomenon, and thus never without a body, disappearing when the body ceases to function. To the ethical idealist this impossibility of the psychological immortality is a revelation; for such pseudo-immortality could satisfy only the low and vulgar instincts of man, and not his ethical feelings. Only to a cheap curiosity can it appear desirable that the inner life viewed as a

series of psychological facts shall go on and
on, that we may be able to see what is to happen in a thousand or in a million years. Life
seen from a psychological point of view as a
mere chain of psychological phenomena is utterly
worthless. It would be intolerable for seventy
years; who would desire it for seventy million
years? Multiplication by zero always leads
back to naught. And even if we perceive all
the facts of the universe for all time to come, is
that of any value? We should shiver at the
thought of knowing all that is printed in one
year, or all that men of a single town feel pass-
ing through their minds; how intolerable the
thought of knowing even all that is and that
will be! It is like the thought of endlessness in
space: if we were to grow endlessly tall, so that
we became large like the universe, reaching with
our arms to the stars, physically almighty, would
our life be more worth living, would it be better
or nobler or more beautiful? No; extension in
space and time has not the slightest ethical
value, for it necessarily refers only to those
objects which exist in space or time, and all our
real values lie beyond it. The mortality of the
psychological phenomena and the immortality of
our real inner life belong necessarily together,
and the claim that the deceased spirits go on
with psychological existence is therefore not
only a denial of the purposes for which the idea

of psychological existence is constructed, but also a violation of the ethical belief in immortality.

Here, then, as everywhere, mysticism means nothing else than the attempt to force the emotional categories on an unreal construction, whose only presupposition was that it had to be constructed as an unemotional objective mechanism. The result is a miserable changeling, which satisfies neither the one side nor the other. If mysticism is not contented with the childish or hysteric pleasure of throwing obstacles in the way of advancing science, it can have, indeed, little satisfaction from its own crippled products. Thousands and thousands of spirits have appeared; the ghosts of the greatest men have said their say, and yet the substance of it has been always the absurdest silliness. Not one inspiring thought has yet been transmitted by this mystical way; only the most vulgar trivialities. It has never helped to find the truth ; it has never brought forth anything but nervous fear and superstition.

We have the truth of life. Its realities are subjective acts, linked together by the categories of personality, giving us values and ideals, harmony and unity and immortality. But we have, as one of the duties of life, the search for the truth of science which transforms reality in order to construct an impersonal system, and gives us causal explanation and order. If we force the system of science upon the real life, claiming that our life is really a psychophysical phenomenon, we are under the illusion of psychologism. If, on the other hand, we force the views of the real life, the personal categories, upon the scientific psychophysical phenomena, we are under the illusion of mysticism. The result in both cases is the same. We lose the truth of life and the truth of science. The real world loses its values, and the scientific world loses its order; they flow together in a new world controlled by inanity and trickery, unworthy of our scientific interests and unfit for our ethical ideals.

INDEX

INDEX

6010246R10169

Printed in Great Britain
by Amazon.co.uk, Ltd.,
Marston Gate.